MW01489530

1

Way Off Base

By Matt Mosler

ISBN 978-0-977-9340-0-3

Published by
High Point Publishers, Inc.
813 Oak Street, Suite 10A-310
Conway, AR 72032

In Cooperation with
Beautiful Feet Ministries, Inc.
3 Trent Jones Cove
Sherwood, AR 72120
www.beautifulfeetministry.com

Cover Photography
Guy Lyons
www.kaiographics.com

Cover Design
Bill Tibbett
Jenkins Enterprises
7200 Industry Drive
North Little Rock, AR 72117
www.jenkins-enterprises.com

ISBN: 978-0-977-9340-0-3

For Travis, Madison & Rebecca

May you continue to grow into the men and women God created
you to be

For Camille

I'll always cherish the treasure of you

CONTENTS

Chapter One

Tag

Do you remember playing tag? I know it's probably been a long time for some of you but if you can think back to simpler days you'll probably remember that the object of the game was to tag as many people as you could without being tagged yourself, right? Because when you're tagged then you're "it" and it's not good to be "it." You may also remember what you did when you got tired or thirsty or needed to renew your strategy. You went to base didn't you?

Base. Base was a great place. Base could be a pole or a tree or a patch of grass or the side of the math building. Whatever it was, base was a safe zone where you could catch your breath, renew your energy and maybe draw up a new plan of attack. But if you wanted the game to continue you knew you couldn't stay at base, right? Eventually you'd have to take a deep breath, scope out the crowd and get right back into the game...and tag as many people as possible.

Imagine what would have happened, though, if instead of heading back out onto the playground you decided to stay at base. Then you invited other players to stay with you. Soon there were a whole bunch of people standing around a flagpole. What if someone then decided that, you know, base would be a lot more comfortable if instead of standing we could sit? So someone decided to add some chairs and sofas. What if so many people started coming to that base because it was so comfortable that they ran out of room? What if someone then decided that in order for everyone to be safe and comfortable at base they were going to have to build a really huge one right there in the middle of the playground so everyone could see how really cool it was?

But what would happen if all those people, safe and comfortable at the really cool base, started to get bored? What if instead of heading back outside to play tag someone thought it would be a lot less dangerous to instead fill the base with toys and games and food? Soon a host of base dwellers would jump and laugh and eat and have fun, right? But what would happen if others began to grumble? What if they thought they had a better way to keep the base dwellers happy?

What if other bases soon began to pop up and compete with the really cool base? What if those other bases offered more games and more toys and more food and some even opened what seemed like entire amusement parks all for the base dwellers enjoyment? Well, the base dwellers would become base jumpers wouldn't they? They would jump from base to base trying to satisfy the boredom they felt but never really finding an answer for that niggling feeling inside them that there was more to the game than even the coolest bases had to offer.

What if all these bases began to notice they were spending an awful lot of money trying to keep the base jumpers from jumping? What if, in order to keep their numbers up, they began to accuse the other bases of not being "true" bases and look down upon those who decided to dwell elsewhere? And what of those who just wanted to play tag again? Would they be ostracized, made fun of, labeled as radical, disloyal or extreme? What if the bases got so sidetracked trying to build bigger and better bases with more fun and games for the base jumpers that they totally lost sight of the reason for the base in the first place?

And what of those other kids on the playground? What if they noticed that spending time in all those different bases wasn't really making a difference in the lives of those base jumpers? What if they ignored the pithy signs on the highways and stayed home because no one wanted to play with them anyway? What if they watched the bases grow larger and more active all while becoming

increasingly

more

irrelevant?

I'm sure that would never happen. I just wonder…

BACK TO BASICS

You know, when you strip away all of the rituals and customs and religion that has been built up around Jesus' words we as his followers are left with a pretty clear command: Go.

"All authority has been given to me in Heaven and on earth. Go, therefore and make disciples of all the nations, baptizing them in the name of the Father and the Son and the Holy Spirit, teaching them to observe all that I commanded you; and lo, I am with you always, even to the end of the age." (Matt. 28:18-20)

Our job is to go…outside the walls of our church and meet people where they are. We are to share the love of Christ with them. We are to welcome them into our fellowship. We are to teach and mentor and disciple them. Then we are to encourage them to lather, rinse and repeat.

I don't think I can see this any more clearly than Pastor Robert Lewis did a few years back. Lewis is one of the founders and the former senior pastor of Fellowship Bible Church in Little Rock, Arkansas. He's also the creator of the very popular devotional series, Men's Fraternity. In a sermon Lewis gave to his congregation on March 19th, 2006 called "Go People" he explained that Jesus was indeed a fisher of men but the type of fishing he practiced was catch and release; he caught them, he discipled them then he released them back into the river. But the type of fishing most of us employ these days, Lewis explained, is catch and keep. We catch people then throw 'em in the live well and try to come up with all sorts of church programs that will keep them entertained. But you know what happens to fish in the live well, Lewis asked? They die. Christian fish, he said, are meant to live in the river.

See, I told you I couldn't say it any better than that.

8

And you see a perfect picture of this when you study the relationship between Jesus and his disciples. Have you ever noticed where Jesus found his disciples? Peter and Andrew were fishing as were James and John (Matt. 4:18-21), Matthew was conducting business in his tax office (Mt. 9:9), and he found Philip and Nathaniel while he was walking to Galilee (Jn. 1:43-48). Now I suppose Jesus could have set up a nice tent with a steeple on top and a flashing sign in front but he chose instead to meet people where they were; working and walking and living.

He spent the next several months, maybe longer, teaching them. They heard him speak (Lk. 6:20-49), they watched him heal the sick (Luke 7:9-10), and raise the dead (7:15), and break down social barriers (7:36-50). They witnessed him display power over storms (8:22-25), and over demons (26-39) and once again over sickness and death (45-56). And after Jesus felt that his disciples had seen and heard enough he sends them out on their own. Well, sort of.

After he gathers them together one day he instructs them on their mission, *"Preach, saying, 'The kingdom of heaven is at hand.' Heal the sick, raise the dead, cleanse the lepers, cast out demons, freely you received, freely give."* (Mt. 10:8) In other words, *"All those things you've seen and heard me do...now it's your turn!"* But He didn't send them out unprepared and he didn't send them out entirely alone. The Bible says, *"He gave them authority!"(Mt. 10:1)* Who's authority? HIS authority! They were caught, they were discipled and they were released in order to make new disciples. And you know what? It worked! Mark 6 picks up the story in verse 30, *"And the apostles gathered together with Jesus; and they reported to Him all that they had done and taught!"*

Can't you sense the excitement there! Don't you wish you could have been there to see these fishermen and businessmen and laborers all coming together talking about the bodies that were healed and the souls that were delivered and the lives that were changed in the authority of

Jesus! Don't you wish you could experience something like that? Well, the kicker is...you can! In fact you're expected to!

See, if you call yourself a believer in Jesus, if you've accepted his free gift of salvation, then you've been caught. If you've spent anytime in Sunday school, or small group or learning more about who he is and what he's done for you then you're being taught. And just like those disciples of old you, too, are being sent. The problem is so few of us will ever get a sense of what those disciples felt and experienced because we're just so safe and comfortable on base.

Don't think so? Then let me ask you a really stupid question. *Should you invite a non-believing person to church?* See, I told you it was stupid. Of course you should, right? Well, here's another stupid question then. *Why?*

Of course church is not an exclusive club where we check IDs and only members are allowed (at least it shouldn't be) and everyone is welcome to come in and see how the body of Christ operates. A non-believer would surely benefit by watching how we interact with each other in love and hopefully they would be inspired by seeing how different and joyful our lives are but that's not really the purpose of church.

Look, what is the definition of church? A body of...believers, right?

See, the church is a gathering place for people who already profess Jesus Christ as their savior. The church is a collection of people who've already pledged their lives to furthering His gospel. The church is supposed to be a place where everyone already knows Jesus is the son of the living God who died for their sins and has a purpose and a plan for their lives. So why would you invite an unbeliever to this gathering?

The purpose of church as Jesus demonstrated and the writer of Hebrews explained is to, *"stimulate one another to love and good deeds, not forsaking our own assembling together, as is the habit of some, but encouraging one another; and all the more; as you see the day drawing near."* (Heb. 10:24-25) Paul tells the young pastor Timothy that church is to be a place where believers can go to *"pursue righteousness, faith, love and peace with those who call upon the Lord from a pure heart."* (2 Tim. 2:22)

Just like base in the game of tag, church is where we go to get our batteries charged, our bodies healed, and our spirits renewed. But just like in the game we were never intended to stay there. If we ever hope to live the life God created us to live we're going to have to get off base and back in the game.

Now, I know some of you think I'm nuts so let me have one more crack at this before you throw this book away.

GATES

Do you remember that passage where Jesus asks Peter, *"But who do you say that I am?"* And Peter responds with, *"Thou art the Christ, the Son of the living God."* (Mt. 16:15-17) It was a pretty big moment for Peter because then he hears Jesus say, *"Blessed are you, Simon Barjona, because flesh and blood did not reveal this to you but My Father who is in heaven. And I say to you that you are Peter, and upon this rock I will build my church; and the gates of Hades shall not overpower it."* (17-18)

Most of my life I thought that meant that if I professed Jesus Christ as my savior I would get a great big target on my back and Satan and all his minions would unleash Hell and all its wrath in order to keep me from becoming the person God created me to be. But because I was a believer I would be able to hunker down behind that shield of faith and be saved from all those flaming darts the enemy threw my way. I thought Jesus would dig me a big foxhole for me and the angels would cover me with their wings to make sure I would be able to withstand the power of the evil one.

11

That's what I believed. Until I read that verse again and noticed one little word: "gates." Do you see it now? Here's why that little word is so important.

You know in the last several decades the United States has been involved in several wars and military conflicts. And in each of these the media has been able to have cameras embedded on the battlefield. This means that each night on TV or at any hour on the internet we've had the ability to see the battles waged in living color. Now, thinking back on all the TV you've watched since you were a little kid do you ever remember one side attacking another side with a gate? Have you ever heard of a thermonuclear gate? Do they build rocket propelled gates? No. Why, because gates are defensive. Gates are meant to keep people out.

The gates of Hell are holding captive God's children and have been for far too long. What Jesus is telling Peter is that as a follower of Christ, as a disciple of the Rabbi, as a soldier in the service of the King Peter needs to take that life saving revelation that Jesus is the Messiah, the son of the living God and the savior of the world and charge the gates of Hell! We are to break down barriers, proclaim release to the captives and set free those who are downtrodden. We, as followers of Christ, are to take the offensive! And there's no way that Satan even with the power of every demon at his disposal has the ability to stop OUR onslaught!

That's good stuff right there!

We must stop inviting people into our churches so someone else can share the gospel with them. That's our job out there! Stop expecting your pastor to do all the preaching. Stop expecting your music minister to do all the worship. Stop expecting your missionaries to do all the evangelism. We all make up the body of Christ. Stop being spectators in this divine dance and start being active participants. Once we share the gospel with those with whom we come into contact then we can bring them into the fellowship so they can receive all the encouragement, stimulation, motivation, accountability, mentoring, comforting and all those other things that the body of believers is supposed to supply.

Look, I love base. Base is a wonderful place. But it was never meant to be our home. That journey of life, outside the walls, that's our home.

So let's go ye therefore. Let's get off base. And play tag!

Section One

The Call

Chapter Two

Letting Go

"What if I stumble, what if I fall?
What if I slip and I make fools of us all?"
-DC Talk

"What if I fail?" he said with tears in his eyes. *"So many others have tried to do what I feel in my heart God wants me to do. What will they say if I mess it up?"*

"I can't do this," she said. *"I'm way out here on a limb and I don't think I have the ability to do what I feel God wants me to do."*

"Brother, I need you to pray with us." He said. *My wife feels God wants her at home full-time and I don't know if we can afford it."*

And thus begins the journey.

The people who made these exact statements to me may not have realized it at the time but they had just uttered the opening words to every great success story: *"I can't do it, God. I need your help!"*

Getting off base is no easy feat. Over time it can become a pretty comfortable place to be. I mean, we have the chairs just the way we like them. The music is hip. They even moved the time up so we can be the first ones to the Golden Corral. And yet…something's missing.

I wonder what thoughts went through Peter's mind as he watched his best friend and Lord ascend into that cloud and go back to his Father. It had only been a few days since Jesus had said to him, ***"Simon, son of John, do you love me? Tend my sheep."*** (Jn. 21:17) As he walked down that mountain he may have thought, *"Sure, it's easy to be brave when the Son of God is walking with you but now he's gone. How in the world am I supposed to be 'the rock?' How am I supposed to tend these sheep when I have enough trouble tending to myself?"*

I'm sure he was afraid but after denying him once Peter wasn't about to run from Jesus again. He and the other disciples went into that upper room and began to pray. Ten days later the power that Jesus promised them, the power that would enable them to fulfill their calling came rushing in like a mighty wind. Soon, Peter, ***"taking his stand with the eleven,"*** *(Acts 2:14)* made his way down to the street and with the power of the Holy Spirit was transformed into the person God created him to be.

Times had definitely changed. The outpouring of the Holy Spirit wasn't just for the priests anymore. It wasn't just for the prophets or the kings. God said he would "***pour out his Spirit upon all mankind: upon his sons and his daughters, for the young as well as the old, and for the servants as well as the wealthy.***" (Acts 2:17-18) He poured out his spirit on a rag tag bunch of disciples 2000 years ago and yes, folks, it's still God's desire to continue pouring out his spirit upon you today.

My friend Jimmy hadn't been saved but a few years when he felt God calling him to start a men's retreat in his area. He was aware most everyone knew what the old Jimmy was like. Why should they listen to him now? But Jimmy prayed. He made himself available. He sought Godly counsel and encouragement and enduring the ridicule and the doubts of others he stepped out in faith and that first retreat drew nearly 500 men.

The truth is, God doesn't expect you to be able to do what he's called you to do. Peter had never walked on water before. Noah had never built a boat. Heck, Noah had never seen rain! And Moses? Moses wasn't just slow of speech he was also wanted for murder when God told him to demand that Pharaoh release the slaves. Think about it, if these guys could do what God called them to do then who would get the glory?

How about this, salvation through Christ was the most important message the world had ever received. It was critical that God's message of faith and hope be shared with everyone around the globe. So who did he trust with this vital piece of information? The rabbinical scholars of his day? The political power brokers? No. He surrounded himself with swindlers, prostitutes, zealots and brash, smelly fishermen among others. Well qualified? Heavens no. Not in their own strength but by making themselves available to the power of God's Holy Spirit they became world changers. And so can you!

MY STORY

I'll never forget the moment I felt God calling me out of my boat. It was in the fall of the year 2000. I was sitting in the choir loft of my church in North Little Rock, Arkansas. There was a missionary in the pulpit that day. To be honest I'm not really sure what he said, all I know is that in the middle of the service I heard God tell me in a very high tenor voice that it was time to get out of television and follow him into ministry …and I said no. I mean, c'mon. Ministry? How would I make a living at that? Seriously, I trusted God with my eternal salvation I just didn't trust Him with my house payment!

See, up until that moment I had spent my entire professional career as a television reporter, host and meteorologist. I loved my job. And for nearly 15 years it defined me. At the time of "the calling" I was the co-host of the top rated morning show in the state and by market share one of the top rated morning shows in the county. Because of my "celebrity" I was invited to dozens of schools and churches and civic groups every year where I was not only able to promote the show but also to share my testimony. It seemed God had me in the perfect place to do His will. I was popular, prosperous and in total control. So why was I asking God every night if this was all there was to the Christian life?

It was around September of 2000 that I began to feel a stirring. It was sort of reminiscent of that scene in the movie *Dances with Wolves* when

Kevin Costner hears and feels the rumble of the buffalo for the first time. He doesn't know what it is, but he knows it's something significant and he's got to find out more. My heart told me that God was trying to prepare me for something big. I shared this sensation with a men's accountability group that I met with once a week and asked them to pray for me. You have to understand that with my inflated, overconfident ego and my Americanized view of Christianity I'm thinking this stirring means God's about to get me an offer from *Good Morning America* or a big recording contract.

It was also about this time that the manager of the local Christian bookstore recommended I read, The Prayer of Jabez, by Bruce Wilkinson. Boy, did that book open my eyes. As I understood it, all Jabez wanted to do was be in a position to make a mark for God. He wanted God to bless him with more opportunities so that he could use those opportunities to have a greater impact for the kingdom. Man, that was me! As quickly as I could, I got down on my knees and prayed, *"Lord bless me indeed! Expand my borders. Keep your hand upon me and keep me from evil so that I may not cause any pain. Amen!"*

In retrospect, I can't say that my passion for television disappeared overnight, but it wasn't very much later. At first I thought it was just a passing phase, that I was tired or frustrated with the direction of my show and my career. But as time went on my desire only deepened. All I could think about was being behind a pulpit or finding other ways to minister to people. I began to get the sense that I wasn't doing what I was supposed to be doing.

My contract was coming up in a couple of months, and I knew I would have to make a decision soon. My heart was telling me to step away from my job and follow him in faith. But, look, I'm a coward by nature. I've never been a big risk taker. I mean I'll take chances as long as I'm sure about the outcome, right? I couldn't just quit my job and trust God to meet my needs, could I? I can't tell you how desperately I wanted to take the step out of the boat but I just didn't have that kind of faith. I needed some encouragement.

So I began dropping hints to my wife that perhaps it was time to do something else or explore other options, you know, like something in the ministry, maybe…sort of…I don't know I'm just thinking out loud here. She wasn't real supportive of the idea, to say the least, but y'all just don't understand how little those people you watch on TV get paid. I mean, my wife must have been blinded by love when she left a very good paying job as a hair stylist to follow me on this televised journey. I was making just 12-grand a year when we got engaged and right after the ceremony we moved to Jackson, Mississippi and the hefty paycheck of 16-Gs. It got a little better in Austin, Texas and by the time we made it to Little Rock we finally felt like we were healed.

I was finally getting paid enough to give mom and dad back most of the furniture we were borrowing and Camille was able to get rid of all of those old dresses from the '80s, you know, the ones with the shoulder pads and the doilies around the neck? Anyway, things were just starting to get better. In fact after just ten years of marriage we were, at last, able to open our very first savings account! And then I walk in with the, "I-feel-God-wants-me-out-of-television-and-into-full-time-ministry" blast. Not the best timing in the world.

Maybe I was just frustrated. Maybe I wasn't quite "in tune" with the voice of God. After all, I wasn't "super Christian". What did I know of the voice of God? I mean, who am I? Maybe I was having, as I was told several times, *a mid-life crisis.* Mid-life? At 34? It was about this time that a local pastor encouraged me to read Wild at Heart, by John Eldredge.

Of the many things that Eldredge touches on in that great book, what got to me the most was his premise that men were created to be a little wild, to take risks, and to live a life of adventure for God's sake as well as their own! It reminded me of that dream sequence early on in the movie, *Braveheart,* when a young William Wallace is staring at the recently slain body of his father. His father looks over at his frightened son and says, *"William, your heart is free. Have the courage to follow it."*

Whoa. What I wouldn't give for the courage to follow what my heart is telling me to do. It began to dawn on me that perhaps this stirring was indeed God trying to lead me in another direction; a direction that didn't particularly make a whole lot of sense but one in which I knew I needed to follow.

To make a long story…not quite as long…when my contract came up in April of 2001 it was not renewed. Despite having the top rated show in the market, more than the other two stations combined, and despite having high personal ratings in the state my news director told me that Wednesday morning, *"Matt, the ratings appear to be slipping, we think you're making too much money, and we're going to take the show in a new direction. You've just worked your last show at this station."* I say in stunned silence for nearly a minute. Then I felt something rumbling way down deep inside me. It began to work its way up. I tried to hold it back but I couldn't. Despite my best efforts to maintain my professional composure I couldn't help but burst out all over the room, *"Well, praise God!"*

There are times I wished I'd had the courage to resign, but it just wasn't in me. I could see Jesus standing out there in the deep water waving at me saying, ***"Be bold, I'm God, don't be afraid!"(Paraphrased from Matt 14:27)*** And even though my heart was racing across those waves to embrace Him, it was hard to make my body let go of that money and those benefits and that security and that position and that power. In truth, I didn't step out of the boat…I was kicked out! But here I am. And there you are.

Many of you know exactly what I'm talking about. You put on a brave face in public, but when the lights are out and the TV is turned off, and praise God the kids have gone to sleep, you feel it, don't you? You feel that same stirring in your heart. But could the God of all creation really be trying to get through to you? Why not? Folks, we have to begin to understand that God has no higher priority than seeking and saving all those souls that he so carefully created in secret (Psalm 139). That was Jesus' mission when he walked the earth as the body of Christ (Luke

19:10). And unless Fox News has missed the biggest story in the history of the world I don't believe Jesus is still walking around on the earth today…but his body is. Ephesians 1:23 and 4:12, among others, says we, the church, are now 'The Body.' Yeah, the body may have changed but the mission hasn't. The purpose of the body of Christ is still to *"seek and save that which is lost."*(Luke 19:10) And until we embrace that mission, no matter what we do, we will never be content.

Now, many of you sense that it might really be God who's trying to get through to you, but you're afraid to listen. You're afraid because you've built a world that is so safe and secure and controlled that to just walk away now would be foolish even though after living this life for as long as you can remember you're like the rich, young ruler asking Jesus night after night, *"What am I still lacking?"(Matt 19:20)* You're afraid because you think that if you surrender control of your life and step out into the unknown world of faith that number one, God won't be able to meet your needs, and number two, you're kind of afraid of what He's going to ask you to do.

Scary, isn't it? And yeah, when you take that step of faith they're going to laugh at you. And sometimes that laughter comes from the most unlikely of sources. Like I said before, when I told others that I felt God telling me to get out of television and into some kind of ministry I didn't have one person in my church, my family or my circle of friends who said, *"You're not crazy. If you feel this is what God is telling you to do then you go, brother. And I got your back!"* Not one. Instead most people thought I was nuts. But you know, they laughed at Jesus, too.

Remember the story in Mark 5 where Jesus is told that Jairus' daughter has already died so there was no sense in coming to the house. Jesus wasn't swayed. Instead he walks into the house, looks at the crowd of professional mourners assembled and says, *"Why all the ruckus? The child isn't dead she's only asleep."* (Paraphrased from 5:39) And they laughed at him…until that little girl got up and started walking around. They laughed at Noah, too…until the rains came. (Gen. 6 & 7) Well folks, the rain's coming. And you know as well as I that unless we warn our families, our friends and our communities they are going to die in the judgment to come.

That's why God has begun to stir within you. That's why he's calling you into this crazy ministry that's been on your heart. And I know that while every part of you wants to answer the call it's so tough because everyone else around you is telling you to, *"Take a vacation"*, or to *"refocus"*, or to *"just get over it"*. *"It's just a phase."* *"This too shall pass."* But it doesn't, does it? Well listen, faith is nothing if not a risk. Unless you're willing to take a chance and pursue that desire with passion, regardless of the fears of those around you, you will continue to settle for a cheap imitation of the abundant life that Jesus created for you. (John 10:10)

I don't claim to be the sharpest knife in the drawer. I didn't go to seminary. I can't read Greek or Latin. Listen, I spent my whole professional career as a TV meteorologist which means I didn't have to be right but I still got a check! But I'm here, outside the boat in the deep water of faith and let me tell you something...the water's fine. I know based upon experience that once you step off base you'll discover that Jesus is a lot easier to find out on the playground than even in the most comfortable of bases.

This journey upon which you are about to embark is not an easy one. But my prayer for you is the same prayer that Jethro had for Moses. When Moses tells his father-in-law, who's also his boss, that God told him to go back to Egypt and tell the most powerful man on earth to release his slaves Jethro didn't scold him. He didn't call him crazy. He didn't call him irresponsible. He didn't worry about who was going to look after his goats. He looked him right in the eye and said, ***"Go, and peace be with you!" (Ex. 4:18, The Message)***

Chapter Three

How do you know?

"Is your father a ghost or do you converse with the Almighty?"
"In order to find his equal an Irishman is forced to talk to God."
                                    -Stephen speaking to
                                    Hamish in Braveheart.

O.K. First things first. There are a lot of voices out there. How do you know that little voice your hearing or that little stirring inside your heart is really God? How did I know when I was sitting in that choir loft that it was really Jehovah God telling me to get out of television? And don't you get a little nervous when you hear people talking about hearing from God?

The above quote is a line from one my favorite movies, Braveheart. If you recall the scene you'll remember that everyone around Stephen thought he was crazy, not because he talked to God but because he admitted that God actually talked back to him. And if you ever tell anyone that you're starting to hear from God most likely they'll think you're crazy, too. As Erwin McManus writes in his book, The Barbarian Way, *"Every devout believer- in fact, any person of faith from any religious persuasion, whether Christian, Muslim, Buddhist, Hindu, or whatever- believes in prayer, but we all know prayer is supposed to be us talking to God. We get a little nervous when someone starts hearing from God."*

So how do you know? Well, I'm not sure I'm qualified to share with you 'Matt's 7 surefire steps to understanding the voice of God' but Jesus says in John 10:27 that, *"My sheep hear my voice, and I know them and they follow me."* So maybe if we want to understand more clearly the voice of the shepherd we need to act more like his sheep. And how do the sheep know the shepherd's voice? They hang around the guy 24-7.

They're together day and night, rain or shine, through good times and bad. The more time the sheep spend with the shepherd the easier it is for them to distinguish his voice from any other voice that happens to come along and the more apt they are to follow when the shepherd calls them.

So the easy answer, if you want to know for sure that the voice you're hearing is really God's, is to spend as much time as possible with Him. One way to do that is spend more time in prayer, but not the kind of prayer that many of us practice today. I mean if the only time you bow your head is to ask God to bless your food then you're robbing yourself of some really great quality time with the shepherd.

QUIET TIME

Too many of us have turned prayer into a 24-hour all request line when it was meant to be a conversation. Imagine if you walked up to your mother and talked to her like you talk to God.

"Mom, I've got a problem and I need your help. My job is stressing me out and my kids are driving me crazy. What can I do to restore some peace to my life?"

"Well, dear..."

"Thanks Mom. Gotta go."

Man, if I'd have acted like that with my mom she would have torn me up. My mom was old school. She didn't believe in time out. She believed in wear out! It didn't matter where we were, in school, at the mall, at the doctor's office, it mattered not. If you broke the rules she'd grab a shoe or a spoon...heck she'd grab the belt off of a stranger to reinforce her rules.

No, one of the reasons so many of us have trouble hearing from God is that we just don't slow down long enough to wait for the answers to our questions. We need more quiet time but I've got to confess I've never

24

been very good at quiet time. See, when I was a kid I was told by my Sunday school teachers that quiet time was grabbing my Bible and going into a room or a closet and getting alone with God. I tried that but my mind kept wandering and it was hard for me to sit still for very long. So I dropped it. I tried to pick it up as I got older and was able to discipline myself a little better to sit still for longer periods of time but there was still no joy in it. So I changed the definition.

Today some of my best quiet times occur while I'm driving. Think about it…Is there a quieter place on the planet than in your vehicle with the radio turned off? I don't think so. Since I sat down to write this chapter I've had to change the sprinklers, answer the phone, make a few return calls, discipline children and tune out the computer game across the hall. All of this while actually moving to three different rooms looking for "quiet time!" I don't have any of those distractions in my truck. Once I hit the highway there is no better place to open up, confess my sins, sing praises to God and receive grace and mercy, as well as marching orders, from the King of Kings. That's why I love to drive.

By the way, this is called "quiet time" for a reason. Which means when you get in your car or truck DON'T TURN ON THE RADIO! I have friends who can't drive from point A to point B no matter the distance without turning on the stereo so I know for some of you this will be very tough. You might even have to gradually wean yourself off the radio but I promise you, if you're looking for quiet time one of the quietest places on the planet is inside your vehicle without the noise of the radio. Even if it's so-called Christian music it's still noise. It's still a distraction. It will still keep you from tuning in the voice of the shepherd.

I didn't always like silence but I've grown to appreciate solitude. I don't ever want to be lonely but I love to be alone with God. It's in those quiet times that we come face to face with our fears; we see who we really are and where we fall short. I remember once, when I was a boy, driving in a car with my uncle Thommy. His car engine was making some funny sounds so I asked him what that rattle was. He looked at me, turned up the radio and said, "What rattle?" Isn't that what many of us do with the problems in our life, turn up the noise to quiet the rattle?

Priscilla Presley wrote in her autobiography that Elvis always had to have the TV on. The noise of the television had to be there whether anyone was watching or not. I find myself doing that sometimes. If it's not the television it's the radio. Why are we so uncomfortable with silence? Could it be that we're afraid of what we'll hear when there's nothing to drown it out? Silence can be uncomfortable but oh so necessary.

But if silence isn't your issue then maybe what's keeping your from hearing the shepherd is your frenetic pace of life.

SLOW DOWN

We are in such a hurry, aren't we? We practically live in our cars. We eat, sleep, shop and do our banking all within the comfort of our SUV's. My generation is never here we're always on the way somewhere else. Not too long ago Camille sent me to the store to buy some groceries. She must have been tied up doing everything else in house to ask me because she knows I'm a terrible shopper. I mean, she will spend ten minutes looking at labels and comparing volume counts in order to save a couple of pennies while I'll just grab the name brand and go. Anyway, while I'm cruising down the aisle with list in hand I spotted a product that so accurately described my generation to a T that I had to buy it. It was a box of "microwavable" Minute Rice!

When I was a kid, rice took 20-30 minutes to cook. Then they came out with Minute Rice which cut the time to about 5 minutes. Now we're too busy for that! I mean if we can't nuke it and have it on the table in 60 seconds or less then to heck with it!

Why are we in such a hurry? Could it be that with all of our hustling and bustling we're trying to outrun the truth? You know as well as I do this will all eventually catch up with us. As the old commercial says, "You can pay me now or pay me later." It's always better sooner rather than later.

Force yourself, if need be, to slow down. Go for a walk. Sit out on the porch. Do whatever it takes now and then to get away from the noise and the hustle and bustle for just a few minutes every day. The Bible says, *"Above all else guard your heart for it is the well spring of life."* (Prov. 4:23) We will have no abundance from which to share with others if we don't take the time to make sure our well is filled and overflowing. Stop working so hard to dig your own well. Draw close to the shepherd and be filled with his river of living water. (Jer. 2:13)

But now some of you have slowed down. Some of you have quiet time that lasts for hours. Some of you have taken sabbaticals and shut yourselves up in cabins out in the woods all to no avail. You still can't get any clear direction from God. With all due respect…I'm not sure God is the problem.

See, I think there are at least three reasons why so many of us today are having a hard time hearing from God. The first is that when it comes right down to it…we just don't want to hear from God.

DON'T WANT TO HEAR

See, if you want to find God, if you want to hear the voice of the shepherd, if you're willing to get quiet, slow down and seek him with all of your heart and soul you'll find him. Why? Because God is looking for you first! In II Chronicles 16:9 God says, *"The eyes of the Lord move to and fro throughout the earth that He might strongly support those whose heart is completely His."* Now that's cool! The awesome God who created the heavens and the earth, the towering mountains and the beautiful valleys, also created us and desires fellowship with us! The Bible says, *"You will seek the Lord your God, and you will find Him if you search for Him will all your heart and soul."* (Deut. 4:29) What a great promise that is.

27

I think the best place to find God is, of course, in his Word. He is the Word of God. He is Faithful and True but some of us have wandered. Some of us have gone astray and just don't know or are too scared to turn around and run back to him. In that case I believe that if your heart is tender and receptive and you're seeking after him God will reveal himself to you and often times right where you are. In other words, if you like movies, God will reach your heart through some of the movies that you see. If its books you like then God will show himself in the words that you read. And they don't necessarily have to be "Christian" books or movies or even television shows. Now before you think I've jumped on the new age band wagon, hear me out. Remember, if God could speak to Balaam through a donkey (Num. 22:21-30) surely he can use the modern day media (insert your own donkey joke here.)

One of the encouraging nuggets I carry around with me is something I saw on an episode of M*A*S*H way back in the mid-80's. It was an episode where BJ Hunnicut was doing something noble and some cynical army guy asked him if he really thought he could change the world and BJ replied, *"No, just my little corner of it."* I believe God sent that word to me at just the right time. There's so much evil in the world that if we try to get it all we'll get frustrated at our lack of success and quit. But if we put one beautiful foot in front of the other the next thing we know we've walked a thousand miles.

I also felt God speak to me through a movie called, *Chocolat.* I didn't see this movie when it made its rounds through the theaters because it was marketed as kind of a "sex" movie. And like all good Christians we're not supposed to go to the theater and see those kinds of movies...so we rent them. Actually, the movie was recommended by a friend, who thought I would like the message the movie sends about the church. I did. According to the writers, the church is represented by a bunch of gray, shadowy, unhappy, restless, hypocrites who try very hard not to have fun and work even harder to make sure others don't either. Then this woman, dressed in bright red and full of life, enters the town and begins making chocolate. The sweet cocoa quickly becomes a secret, "sinful" pleasure for many of the townsfolk but the woman, who spurns church, is never quite accepted into polite society.

I won't spoil the rest of the movie, but the question I kept asking myself was why should this woman want any part of church? Yes, she needs salvation, but she shouldn't be made to feel that she has to surrender life and joy to get it! Harsh, maybe, but its a little closer to the truth than many would like to admit. Peter said we *"should be ready at a moment's notice to testify of the hope that lives within us." (I Peter 3:15)* When was the last time you were asked to testify of the hope within you? That statement presupposes that we need to live our lives in such a way that others will see that hope within us and realize they need what we have! But I digress...

The point is that God is not hard to find. Romans 1:20 says, *"His invisible attributes, His eternal power and divine nature, have been clearly seen, being understood through what has been made."* The problem is not, "where is God?" The problem is where are you? Are you seeking after him? Are you trying to hear from God? Do you really want to hear what God has to say about your life? If you're not seeking after him with your whole heart, if you're not renewing your mind daily, if you're not hanging out where God hangs out chances are slim you'll hear him when he speaks.

OUR EARS ARE CLOGGED

The second reason why we may be having trouble hearing the voice of the shepherd is that while we have the ears to hear...they may be clogged!

The Bible says in James 1:21, *"Therefore putting aside all filthiness and all that remains of wickedness, in humility receive the word implanted, which is able to save your souls."* A pastor told me one time that the Greek word for filthiness, which is *rhuparia,* is actually the same word they used for 'ear wax.'

Have you ever had ear wax in your ear so bad that you couldn't hear? I know it sounds gross but my doctor tells me it's true and that some of his patients come to him fearing they'll need a hearing aid only to discover what they really need is a Q-tip! Sometimes in order to hear better we just need to clean out the junk.

Recently I was having trouble with my computer so I called the Dell service number. A nice young man named Shawn answered the phone. I don't think Shawn was his given name. Did you know that when you call Dell and their phones in Austin, Texas are busy that your call rolls over to India? I didn't until this day. In any case Shawn was very helpful although his English dictionary and my southern vernacular were sometimes at odds. *"I'll be with you in just a jiffy"* for example, seemed to cause his wires to cross for just a moment. But we got it all worked out.

I called Shawn to inquire why I couldn't open my Word software. It was working fine that morning so why on earth would it not be working now? Shawn sensed my fear and quickly got that mystery solved. But since it took me quite a while to get a human being on the telephone I took the opportunity to get all my computer issues solved. *"Shawn, why is my computer moving so slowly these days? It used to be lightning fast."*

He wondered if I'd ever cleared out my temporary Internet files. I didn't know I had any Internet files to start with let alone temporary ones. *"Oh, yes,"* he said in his lilting Indio-English. *"Every time you log onto the Internet or visit a new site your computer saves a little bit of that page onto its hard drive. The purpose of this,"* he explained, *"is to help those Internet pages open up faster the next time you visit. But over time, if those files aren't cleaned out, it can really slow up and hamper the effectiveness of your entire system."*

"Well then," I said, *"Guess we'd better clean those puppies out... Uh, Shawn, you still there?"*

"Oh, yes," he sang, *"Let's clean out those puppies."*

I was instructed to go to the 'explorer' logo on my desktop and click my right mouse, scroll down to 'properties' and there I'd find the 'temporary Internet files'. If I click on the 'view files' box I'll be able to see all my temporary files. I was astonished. After what seemed like an eternity my little laptop revealed more than 13-thousand temporary files created from visits to the Internet. No wonder I was moving slowly. All those files were clogging up every other operation on my computer, including my Word. It took nearly 10 minutes but Shawn and I were able to clean up my computer and now it's humming like a 200 horsepower Evinrude. I didn't bother explaining that one to Shawn.

But can you imagine? Every time you visit a site on the Internet, even for the briefest of moments, a little piece is left behind, hidden, under the radar screen, and they're piling up. It may take months or in my case years but one day all of those little bits of information eventually overload your system until they are dealt with. You know where I'm going with this don't you? You may not think there was anything to that movie you saw last week or that book you read in the privacy of your own home or those jokes you heard somebody else tell that you just had to repeat because they were just "so terrible". But those little images, those words, those emotions stay with you. And they, too, often lay in wait, stacking up until before long it seems your whole life is falling down around you and you can't figure out why. Wouldn't it be nice to just pick up the phone and talk to a 'Shawn' to get your system up and running again?

Well, don't expect God to hold you down and clean the gunk out of your ears. James 1:19-21 makes it real clear that our anger, wickedness and pride created this problem and if we want to *"receive the word implanted,"* if we want to hear what God has to say to us then WE have to do the cleaning. But how do we do that? Well, long before Dell opened an office in Asia, God instructed a man named Paul to write a letter to Christians in the town of Philippi encouraging them to fill their minds with whatever is true and honorable and right and pure. *"If you*

do," he says, *"then the God of peace will be with you." (Phil. 4:8-9)*
The converse is also true. If you don't dwell on these things but fill your mind with immorality then God can't possibly bring you peace. As the old saying goes "garbage in, garbage out." If you want the God of peace to have fellowship with you then you have to stop conforming to the world and begin transforming your mind by reading God's word, meditating upon it day and night and beyond that put into practice what you read. If you can do that the Bible promises that we *"will be able to prove what the will of God is for our lives, that which is good and acceptable and perfect."* (Rom 12:2)

God wants you to know his good, acceptable and perfect will for your life and he will never contradict himself. So if you want to know for sure that it's God speaking to your heart then clean out your ears by reading your word because he will always back up what he says.

EARS TO HEAR

But some of you have prayed. Some of you have desperately sought him out. Some of you are spending countless hours in his word and still you don't have any clear direction for your life. Here's one final thought…You may not have ears to hear. (Matt 11:15)

See, God doesn't speak to your flesh, he speaks to you through his Holy Spirit and we can only understand him if we're of the same spirit. *"For who among men knows the thoughts of a man except the spirit of the man which is in him? Even so the thoughts of God no one knows except the Spirit of God. Now we have received, not the spirit of the world, but the Spirit who is from God, that we might know the things freely given to us by God…but a natural man does not accept the things of the Spirit of God; for they are foolishness to him, and he cannot understand them, because they are spiritually appraised."* (I Cor. 2:10-14)

Have you received the Spirit of God into your heart? Do you understand that living your life by your rules is considered rebellion before your creator? God calls that rebellion sin and your sin, your rebellion before the King of the universe, carries the very steep price of eternal death. But God created you for his fellowship. And he loved you so much that even though you rebelled against him he still sent his only son, Jesus, to live a sinless life on earth and become the perfect sacrifice for your sins. (Rom. 5:8) In other words he paid for your rebellion. But he didn't stay dead. He rose from the grave where he now lives at the right hand of God the Father and fights for your daily.

The Bible says if you'll confess your sins before him he'll separate them as far as the east is from the west. (Psalm 103:12, I John 1:9) He'll create within you a new heart. He'll cleanse you as white as snow. (Is. 1:18) He'll make of you a new creature. (2 Cor. 5:17) He'll come in and dwell within you, spirit to spirit. (Rev. 3:20) There will still be a struggle to know his will for your life because evil still abounds in this world and a part of us will always fight to please our flesh but at least we'll have the right number when we want to call upon the Lord.

I would love to be able to say that I always know beyond a shadow of a doubt what God wants me to do and when but it just ain't true. I still wrestle every day discerning his voice. As long as his Holy Spirit dwells in my unholy body I have a feeling I always will but I believe I'm getting better. I don't worry as much today about making mistakes. I don't worry as much today about what other people think. And although it's still a struggle I don't worry as much today about trying to make sense of what I feel God is asking me to do. In fact, if I've learned nothing else since I stepped back out onto the playground it's this: If it makes absolutely no sense at all…it's probably from God.

But now some of you may still be thinking, "Why on earth would God call me? I mean seriously, me?"

Well, why not you? You are fearfully and wonderfully made. God put you together on purpose. He knows best how to use the gifts, talents and abilities he gave you. The Bible says of all the people on the planet Jesus chose you! (Jn. 15:16) And he's calling upon you now to fulfill the ministry he created for you to live. See, in his infinite wisdom God has chosen you to be the vessel through whom many in this world will be saved. And you want to know the real scary part? There is no plan B.

Chapter Four

The Five Excuses of Moses

"I attribute my success to this: I never gave or took an excuse."
-Florence Nightingale

By now there's a pretty good chance that many of you have already heard from God. Call it a stirring, a thought that just won't go away or even an outright dream or vision, the Holy Spirit has been trying to get your attention...and you know it, don't you? Maybe you've tried to ignore the feeling or dismiss it because what you sense you're being asked to do, well, makes absolutely no sense at all. Right? Yeah. Been there.

But, you know, God knows what he's doing and there's a pretty good reason why you're being asked to do things that seem so far beyond your strength, wisdom, knowledge or ability. Think about it. If you could figure out and/or accomplish the impossible task that God is asking you to accomplish then who would get the glory when it's accomplished, Hmmm? Remember, the purpose of our existence is not to glorify ourselves. We've tried that and it's left us wanting. No, our mission is to use our God-given gifts, talents and abilities to draw others to the only one who can save them from their sins.

Now don't worry, God loves you and knows you need a little pat on the back now and then and the Bible says in I Peter 5:6 that He will exalt you in due time. He just doesn't want you exalting you, which is why the calling he will typically put on your life will seem impossible. There's a good chance that stepping out in faith will lead to failure. He will test your will, your endurance and your faith. He'll ask you to do something crazy just like he did Moses out in that Midian desert. (Exodus 3) And because you're afraid you'll probably respond...just like Moses. But

35

listen, if you give in to your fear and continue to run away from the task at hand you will rob yourself of the abundant life God has waiting for you.

So let's tackle Moses' excuses one by one because most likely they will end up being your excuses too. This way you can save a little time and get right to business for both his and your sake.

Excuse #1:   ***"Who Am I?"***

I've never seen a burning bush. Well, I've seen a burning bush but I've never seen one on fire that wasn't burning like Moses did. (Ex. 3:1-4) I bet if I had it would have been easier for me to believe what God was trying to tell me, you know, especially when the bush started talking to me. *"Matt, Matt! It's time to get out of television and get into full-time ministry."*

I would have so believed that was from God and resigned on the spot. I mean you don't see and hear a burning bush every day. But Moses was a little more reticent to follow what the shrub was selling. Look what he says, *"Who am I?"* Good question. Ever ask that one? *Why me? Maybe God's got me mixed up with someone else. Doesn't he know what I've done or what I think? Surely I'm not the best choice to represent Almighty God.* God's answer; ***"Certainly, I will be with you."*** In other words, *"It's not you, Sport. It's me working through you."*

Whom God calls God empowers. No one accused Jesus of picking the cream of the crop for his disciples. Among others, He was hanging out with a rag tag bunch of fishermen, a zealot and a tax collector. But in Matthew 10, Jesus sends these boys out on their first missionary journey...without Him. Well, without Him physically. Their job was to ***"heal the sick, raise the dead, cleanse the lepers, and cast out demons."*** (Mt. 10:8) Don't you think they were a little intimidated? That's God kind of stuff not the work of some guys who just a year or so earlier were sorting fish, inflaming political passions and stealing from their countrymen. But certainly God was with them. Look at verse one, ***"And***

36

having summoned his twelve disciples, he gave them authority…" He gave them authority. Who's authority? His authority. He is Lord of all and He just gave them permission to conduct business in His name!

Now, I have a CPA not because I have a lot of money but because Beautiful Feet Ministry is a non-profit corporation, I'm not very smart and there are a lot of papers that have to be filed properly. So every year I sign a power of attorney that gives my CPA permission to conduct business in my name. When the government sees a document from him they don't see my CPA they see me because he is cloaked with my authority. Jesus did the same thing with those disciples. He cloaked them with his authority which means that sickness didn't see Andrew. That disease didn't take notice of Phillip or Bartholomew. Those demons saw not James or Thaddeus but Jesus! We read later in Mark 6:30, *"The apostles gathered together with Jesus; and they reported to Him all that they had done and taught."* In other words, He gave them his authority and it worked!

Now, here's the cool part. Jesus has given you the very same authority He gave to his first disciples, *"All authority has been given to Me in Heaven and on earth. Go, therefore, and make disciples of all nations, baptizing them in the name of the Father and the Son and the Holy Spirit, teaching them to observe all that I commanded you,"* and here it is again, *"And lo, I am with you always, even to the end of the age."*(Mt. 28:18-20)

You have the same power the disciples had to accomplish what He's called you to do. It's not you, it's Him. Who are you? You are a child of the king with royal rights and privileges. (Rom. 8:15, Js. 2:5) Now start living like it. Go, and fulfill your calling because certainly, He will be with you!

Excuse #2:   *Who Are You?*

"Then Moses said to God, 'Behold I am going to the sons of Israel, and I shall say to them, 'The God of your fathers has sent me to you.' Now

they may say to me, 'What is His name?' What shall I say to them?"
(Ex. 3:13)

For forty years Moses was reared as an Egyptian learning and excelling in their ways and customs. The next forty years of his life was lived in exile herding sheep and goats for his father-in-law. While he had the birthright of a son of Israel he wasn't culturally Hebrew. What did he know of Jehovah and His ways? He didn't even know His name! Shouldn't he wait and learn more about God before he steps into this ministry he's being called to?

How many of us are afraid to become the people God's calling us to be because we don't know Him that well? *"I didn't go to seminary." "I don't read the Bible as much as I should." "I don't even like to pray in public because I'm afraid I'll do it wrong!"* And yet you feel called, don't you.

Listen, knowledge of God is critical but it isn't nearly as important as obedience. The blind man whom Jesus healed in John chapter 9 wasn't even saved when he was asked to testify before the Sanhedrin. Yet there he was boldly proclaiming the only thing he knew about Jesus, ***"Whether He is a sinner, I do not know; one thing I do know, that whereas I was blind, now I see!"*** (9:25) Eventually that man did get to know Jesus on a more personal level (35-38).

Before he became 'The Apostle Paul' the Pharisee Saul was one of the smartest guys on the planet. From the time he was born he had devoted his life to the study of the scriptures (Phil. 3:5-6). Yet when that bright light hits him on the road to Damascus this man with the encyclopedic knowledge of God says, ***"Who art thou, Lord?"*** (Acts 9:5) That's right, even Paul didn't know everything about Jesus. And he never would. Years later he would write to the church at Rome, ***"Oh, the depth of the riches both of the wisdom and knowledge of God! How unsearchable are His judgments and unfathomable are His ways."*** (Rom. 11:33) Knowing about Christ and knowing Christ are two different things.

Look, who did Jesus attack more than any other group in his ministry? The Pharisees, right? And who had more knowledge of the scriptures than they did? Yet time and time again we see Jesus calling them things like a brood of vipers or whitewashed tombs or blind guides of the blind. Why, because *"knowledge makes arrogant, but love edifies."* (I Cor. 8:1) Paul and the rest of the Pharisees knew about Christ but they didn't know Him. It's kind of like reading a biography about someone. You know, you get to learn the facts and figures about their life like when they were born and the jobs they've held but you don't really get to know them. That kind of knowledge can only be gained on a road trip! Nothing really bonds two people together like driving across the country, sleeping in your car and digging through the seat cushions looking for change so you can have your hash browns scattered, smothered and covered.

Now, please don't misunderstand me, the Bible is clear that it should be a top priority of every believer to learn more about Christ everyday. For example, *"Be diligent to present yourself approved to God as a workman who does not need to be ashamed, handling accurately the word of truth."* (2 Tim. 2:15) See also Rom. 12:1-2, Eph. 6, Col. 1:9-10, Heb. 5:12, Jude 3, just to cite a few. But just as you're never really ready to have children neither will you ever be fully ready to follow Christ. Moses didn't think he was ready. He didn't even know God's name when he started his journey but by the time he was finished he knew God face to face (Deut. 34:10).

When God calls; go. You'll figure out the rest as you grow in relationship together.

Excuse #3:   *They'll Think I'm Nuts!*

She knows it's a risk. It's such a crazy idea, anyway. Her community has been in an economic depression for years. Starting a business there, well, no one starts a business there. Especially someone who's never operated a business. So she asked me with a sense of desperation, *"I know this is crazy but I really feel God wants me to open up a beauty school down here and help some of these girls out of their cycle of poverty. Everyone tells me it's a stupid idea. What do you think?"*

"What do I think? I think it's a risk. I think it's a gamble with money you don't have to waste. I think you've never owned or operated a business before. Sounds like God!"

Like so many of us my friend lives a pretty good life. She's a good 'church girl,' well versed in the rules and rites of her faith. She prays, reads her Bible and otherwise walks the straight and narrow road. But like the rich, young ruler she often finds herself asking, ***"What am I still lacking?"*** (Matt. 19:20) She knows there's a greater purpose to her life. Could the answer to her question be something as secular as a beauty school? Perhaps a better question would be, *"Do I have the courage to follow God even though everyone will think I'm nuts?"*

That's the question I asked myself when I felt God calling me to step away from a high profile job and follow Him into an unknown ministry. Moses asked a similar question after God told him to go to the leaders of Israel and tell them He had heard their cries and would soon deliver them from the Egyptians to a land flowing with milk and honey (Ex. 3:17). ***"What if they will not believe me"***, Moses said, ***"or listen to what I say? For they may say, 'The Lord has not appeared to you.'"*** (Ex. 4:1)

Why would they believe him? He's been a goat herder for the past 40 years far removed from the palaces of Egypt. He was never tight with the Jewish leaders anyway and now God, speaking to him from a burning bush that wasn't really burning, was asking him to be their leader? Of course they're going to think he's nuts, right? And that's exactly where God wants us. You know His thoughts are not our thoughts, neither are His ways our ways (Is. 55:8). That's why it's not up to us to understand God, it's just up to us to obey.

Look at how God answers Moses' questions. He has him throw his shepherds staff on the ground where it turns into a snake. Then he tells him to pick up that snake by the tail. Now, Moses had never seen a single episode of The Crocodile Hunter but even he knew picking up a snake by the tail was not very smart. That's why Steve Irwin always had one of those broken off sticks with him. Otherwise that snake could turn right around and ruin your whole day. But God said, *"Stretch out your hand and grasp it by its tail."* (4:4) So suspending all reason, experience and common sense Moses did as God commanded and that snake turned right back into a staff again. Similarly when Moses obeyed God, overcame his fear and shared God's word with the people of Israel, *"the people believed…and they bowed low and worshipped."* (4:31)

Why does God ask us to do such crazy things? Why does God put us in positions where we have to overcome our fear, discount our experience and ignore our common sense? Easy, so that when we accomplish the impossible only He can get the glory. The Bible says if we humble ourselves before his mighty hand He will exalt us at the proper time. (I Pet. 5:6) God wants to exalt you he just doesn't want you to exalt you…because He knows when we go in our strength we end up with a cheap imitation of the abundant life He's called us to. (Jn. 10:10)

So when He calls, go! Don't worry about the 'how.' Just follow and trust Him to take care of the heavy lifting.

Incidentally my friend never started that beauty school. Pity.

Excuse #4:   *I'm Not Qualified*

I know we're not supposed to question such things but have you seriously considered God's plan for saving all mankind? I'm not talking about the sending of his son to pay the penalty for our sins. As fantastic as that is I can wrap my mind around the birth, death and resurrection of Jesus. No, I'm talking about what his plan was from that point on. In short, it goes something like this, *"YOU shall be my witnesses…to the remotest parts of the earth,"* (Acts 1:8) and, *"Go YE therefore and make disciples…"* (Matt. 28:18)

Now, surely God wasn't talking about me when he said ye, was he? Hasn't he heard me speak? Doesn't he know what goes on inside my head? Hasn't he seen the things I've done…or want to do? I ain't no preacher! I'm sure if he's really God he could have come up with a better plan than using someone like me to tell the world how to be saved! But he didn't.

God specializes in using broken people to do His work. He loves calling the castaways. Look what he did with Moses. The man couldn't speak very well. Some scholars say he stuttered. And yet God tells him, *"Gather the elders and SAY to them,"* (Ex. 3:16) and *"You will come to the king of Egypt and SAY to him."* (3:18) Can you really blame Moses for trying to back out of this one? *"G-G-God, I don't talk so g-g-good! Can't you find one of those p-p-preachers with the gold watches to do this?"*

God's funny that way. He takes pleasure in *"destroying the wisdom of the wise and the cleverness of the clever."* (I Cor. 1:19) Instead of a princess he chooses a peasant to be the mother of His only son. He picks a persecutor of the Jews to be their apostle. And going against all the polls he anoints a shepherd boy to be king. Why, *"For God sees not as man sees, for man looks at the outward appearance, but the Lord looks at the heart."* (I Sam. 16:7)

We tend to put a lot of stock in what we perceive are our strengths, talents and abilities yet we forget that it was God who gave all that stuff to us in the first place. He tells Moses, *"Who has made man's mouth? Or who makes him dumb or deaf or seeing or blind? Is it not I, the Lord?"* (Ex. 4:11) God knows what you're made of. And he knows you're potential, too. He knows where you see obstacles he sees opportunities. Where you see limitations he sees limitless possibilities. And where you see giants he sees a boy with a sling shot and five smooth stones.

God chose Moses not for his oratorical skills but because he knew what kind of man he could become if he'd just put his faith in the Lord. So He asks him to do the impossible. He asks Peter to step out of a boat. (Mt. 14:29) He asks the priests to cross the Jordan. (Josh. 3) He tells the disciples to feed 5 to 10-thousand people with just a couple of fish and some bread. (Mt. 14:16) Why, so that they would have to turn to the Lord for strength because as God told Paul, *"My...power is perfected in weakness.*" (I Cor. 12:9) And just as he asked them…he's going to ask you, too!

So few of us will ever come to understand the person we're capable of becoming because we never give God the chance to operate in our lives. We see the size of the mountain and say, *"I can't!"* We look at the waves and say, *"I'm not able."* We gauge the task at hand and say, *"I'm not qualified,"* *"I don't have what it takes,"* *"I'm not spiritual enough,"* *"I've made too many mistakes,"* and nothing ever changes.

God was the one who skillfully wove you together in your mother's womb (Ps. 139). He knows what you're capable of and he didn't call you by mistake. He chose you on purpose to be the vessel through which others may know the love of God. And as I said, there is no plan B.

Excuse #5:   ***Send Someone Else***

Your team is trailing. Time is running out. The game, perhaps even the season, hangs in the balance. You look around at your teammates wondering which one of them is going to take the last shot. Then the coach walks up and hands you the ball.

"Is he kidding? Is this some kind of cruel joke," you wonder? *"Hasn't he seen me play? Doesn't he realize that these other guys are so much better than me? I can't do this! Pick someone else!"*

"No," he explains, *"I choose you. I know what you're made of. I know what you're capable of. I know that if you trust me and just have a little faith we can win this game."*

Moses knew he was outmatched. He knew he didn't have what it takes to stand before Pharaoh and demand the release of his slaves. He knew he was ill equipped to lead 2-million people or more through the desert to freedom. He was just a goat rancher, for goodness sake! And yet God had just handed him the ball and said, ***"Go, and I, even I, will be with your mouth, and teach you what you are to say!"*** (Ex. 4:12)

43

What an incredible promise! God Almighty, the maker of the heavens and the earth, would personally be with Moses, standing beside him, teaching and mentoring him throughout his journey! But Moses didn't hear a word of it or maybe…maybe he didn't believe it. All he saw was the enormous task to which he was being called and cried out, *"Please, Lord, now send the message by whomever thou wilt!"* (Ex. 4:13)

It all comes back to fear, doesn't it? You know, fear is the polar opposite of faith and it's one of the primary tools the enemy uses to keep God's people from fulfilling their potential. If we're afraid of failure or embarrassment or bodily harm or even death then we'll never take the chance to become the person God created us to be. Consider the Israelites in Numbers 13 whose fear caused them to die in the desert rather than possessing their Promised Land. Consider the fear that prevented Jesus from doing many miracles in his own hometown. (Mt. 13:58) Consider the fear that kept Peter from continuing to dance on the white caps. (Mt. 14:30) Fear keeps you in bondage. Faith opens the door to freedom.

God knows what you're made of because he made you! The Bible says in Psalm 139 that he made you in secret; just you and him! He threw in a little of this and a touch of that. He purposefully put you together just the way you are and he did it intentionally. Jer. 29:11 says he has plans for you. Hebrews 12:1 says he's laid before you a race in which you are to run. And in John 15 Jesus says that above anyone else he chose you. He called you. He commissioned you to go, fulfill your ministry and bear fruit. (15:16)

But following God is scary. It was scary for Moses and it will be scary for you, too. The task may seem too great. The giant may seem too large. The mountain…just too imposing. And yet God hands you the ball anyway and says, *"Go, therefore, and make disciples of all the nations, baptizing them in the name of the Father and the Son and the Holy Spirit, teaching them to observe all that I commanded you; and lo, I am with you always, even to the end of the age!"* (Mt. 28:18-20)

You know when you look at that verse and compare it to what God told Moses a few thousand years ago you see it's pretty much the same promise. God made good on that one and you can rest assured Jesus will keep up his end of the bargain with you too. The question is will you give Him a chance to prove He's true to His word?

Time is running out. Our team is trailing. The game is on the line and too many players are content to sit on the sidelines. The coach has His eyes on you. Are you willing to take the ball?

Section Two

Getting in Shape

Chapter Five

Discipline

*"If I had known then how much the gold medal would mean to be today I'd have
hit the bag much longer. I'd have run that much further. I'd have trained that
much harder. If I'd only known.*

-Boxer Jermaine Taylor
Bronze medalist
2000 Sydney Olympics

If I sit real still I can remember what it was like living in Nevada City,
California back in the day lacing up my wallabies and running around the
blacktop at Seven Hills School. It was a pretty good sized playground
but I don't remember ever getting too tired to chase after Kerry
Gallagher. I never caught her but from what I recall she was well worth
the effort.

I doubt that in my present condition I would be able to last more than a
few minutes out on the playground which is a pity since that's where I
feel I'm called to be. I mean, Jesus sat there choosing up sides and
specifically picked me to be on his team. He looked at me and said, *"I
choose you!"* (John 15:16). Wow! Me? That's kind of a big deal.
That sort of inspires me to get in shape…sort of.

Seriously, even though I know God loves me regardless of my deeds and
accomplishments or as some of you might say, "works," I want to be the
best I can be. I want to fulfill my potential. I want to be able to tag
people out on the playground. I want to be in the best shape possible to
run the race and fight the fight and contend earnestly for the faith. And I
know it takes more than just desire to be a follower of Christ. It takes
passion. It takes courage. It takes faith. But maybe what it takes more

than anything else and what makes all those other things more effective…is discipline.

No, no, no…don't go away. Come back!

Yeah, I probably should have titled this something other than "DISCIPLINE!" I know we'd rather hear words like 'grace' & 'freedom' and that God will supply all of your needs, that He will strongly support you, and that he will make you mighty in battle and all that's true but it's also a perversion of God's word to think that the perfect, complete, abundant life God promises is free and doesn't require any effort.

Take a look at Paul's letter to the Ephesians and you'll see what I mean. In just one section between chapters four and five Paul uses words and phrases like, *"Grow up, walk no longer, lay aside, be renewed, put on, speak truth, do not sin, do not let, do not give, let no, do not grieve, be kind, be imitators, walk in love, etc…"* It's silly how many verbs he uses throughout his letters. Verbs as you know denote action. There is some action required of us once we accept the *free* gift of salvation. Getting saved is easy. Jesus has already done all the heavy lifting. All you have to do is accept it and say thank you! Becoming the person God created you to be? Well, just as you can't jump out of your easy chair and run a marathon neither can you achieve your full potential without training and discipline as well as encouragement and accountability. And it begins in the word.

A.   THE WORD

Each of us, no matter where we are in our spiritual walk, needs to be reading our Bibles daily. I'm amazed at the number of churches I visit every year at how few people actually bring their bibles to the service. Growing up I'll never forget my dad having his great, big leather bound Bible with him every Sunday. Of course he kept in the back of the car Monday through Saturday but at least he had it with him in church!

I remember once I received a call from a local lawyer who wanted to meet with me to talk about a stirring he felt God had placed on his heart. He said he'd become more and more convinced over the past several months that God wanted him to become a Bible teacher. I asked him how God had confirmed that emotion in His word since God's voice is always consistent. The man sort of sheepishly looked at me and said, *"Well, I really don't read the Bible all that much."* I guess I should have exercised a bit more compassion and not laughed at him when I said, *"Well, what in the world are you going to teach?"*

It's funny but it's not funny. In what could have easily been a description of our culture the prophet Jeremiah wrote, ***"An appalling and horrible thing has happened in the land: The prophets prophecy falsely, and the priests rule on their own authority; and my people love it so!"*** (Jer. 5:30-31) God's people today are so spiritually malnourished we're unfit for battle which is not good since Paul tells us in Ephesians 6 that we are at war and it's critical that we clothe ourselves in the full armor of God.

Jude calls every believer to ***"contend earnestly for the faith."*** (v. 3) I love that image. Like contenders in a prize fight we not only need to be prepared to fight (1 Pet. 3:15) but also ready at any given moment to defend ourselves (2 Tim. 4:2). But how can we defend our faith when we have no idea what we believe.

Preparing ourselves to defend what we believe is essential to our responsibilities as a believer. It was so important to Jude that instead of writing one letter he felt compelled to write another and appeal to each of us to be contenders or as Paul tells Timothy to ***"fight the good fight of faith."*** (I Tim. 6:12) But so few of us are reading our Bibles that we're not prepared to preach.

The result is that, because of our lack of discipline, our enemy is no longer just outside the church but within. (v.4a) Because we don't know the word and haven't contended for our faith too many churches are not ***"enduring sound doctrine but wanting to have their ears tickled have***

*accumulated for themselves teachers in accordance to their own
desires and have turned away their ears from the truth and have
instead turned aside to myths."* (2 Tim. 4:3-4 paraphrase)

Take for example a sermon I read recently in which the minister stated
that when Jesus said, *"I am the way, the truth and the life"* (John 14:6)
he didn't really mean it. *"Was Jesus actually saying that other religions
who do not know his name are damned? Did Jesus preclude their
possibility of an eternal relationship with the Father? The context of the
scripture tells us otherwise."* The pastor concludes, *"Christianity is not
the only way because clearly others tell us they know God by other
religions."*

Now was that sermon delivered by some kook fringe cult? No. It was
delivered Jan. 8th, 2006 by a pretty prominent church in the heart of the
Bible belt, Little Rock, Arkansas. (www.qqumc.com "Is Christianity the
Only Way?") The danger of not contending for the faith, of not
"retaining the standard of sound words" (2 Tim. 1:13), is that we deny
Jesus as Lord and change grace into a license for immorality. (v.4b) The
result is that God's children either live cheap imitations of the life he
promised them (John 10:10) or they die eternally separated from Him in
Hell!

The solution is simple. Read the word.

Let me share with you an epiphany God gave me in a hotel bathtub
recently. Seriously, for some reason God has chosen bathrooms for
some of my greatest revelations…I don't know why, maybe it's the
solitude. Maybe it's that whole cleansing thing, but I digress. Here
goes…

I was reading near the end of the book of Revelation where John is
describing his vision of the second coming of Christ, *"And I saw
Heaven opened; and behold, a white horse, and He who sat upon it is
called Faithful and True…And he is clothed with a robe dipped in
blood; and His name is called The Word of God."* (Rev. 19:11,13).

I then read just a couple of chapters later that the Christ himself said, *"Write, for these 'words' are faithful and true."* (Rev. 21:5) And again Jesus says in chapter 22 verse 6, *"These 'words' are faithful and true."* So, his name is called Faithful and True and "these words" are faithful and true. That seems just a bit too intentional to be an accident, don't you think?

That forced me to flip back to the gospel of John where the apostle first makes this case when he writes, *"In the beginning was the Word, and the Word was with God and the Word was God...And the Word became flesh and dwelt among us..."* (John 1:1, 14) With this introduction to his gospel John makes it pretty clear that Jesus Christ is the Word. But if you needed just one more verse to be convinced he adds later in his gospel, *"The Word is Truth."* (17:17) And Jesus backs that up by saying, *"I am the Truth..."* (Jn. 14:6)

So, again, his name is called Faithful and True and the words that he speaks and the word that is written is called faithful and true. His name is also called The Word of God and so is that book that we so casually neglect.

I know I may be way behind the curve on all this but I guess I've always looked at my bible as more of a story and less of a personality. It is, after all, the gospel or the "good news" of God's redemption for mankind. The writers of the Amplified Bible say the word is *"the doctrine concerning the attainment through Christ of salvation in the kingdom of God."* (Luke 1:2) And to be sure it *is* a guidebook. It *is* the doctrine of the Christian faith but in light of what I just read I think to say that the word is just the good news...well...sells it short. The Word, as I now understand it...is Christ!"

Now, why am I making such a big deal out of this? Well, maybe it's because after "soaking in" all that information the other day I became convicted that I call myself a Christian yet don't spend near enough time with Christ. And really isn't it the height of arrogance to try to live a Christian life without Christ?

You should know I didn't go to seminary and didn't study this sort of thing in school. And maybe I am being a bit too literal about "the Word being Jesus" but it does stand to reason that if I want to be filled up with Christ that I need to fill myself up with his word. It also make sense that if his Word wasn't so important why then is Satan so steadfast in trying to steal, kill, destroy, pervert, alter and water down the Word? (Mark 4) Maybe he sees the connection more clearly than I do.

The Apostle Paul tells us to *"put on the Lord Jesus Christ,"* to *"lay aside the deeds of darkness and put on the armor of light."* (Rom. 13:14) He makes it clear in Ephesians 6 that the armor of which he speaks is indeed the word of God. Jesus clothed himself in this armor in the wilderness (Matt 4) and we would do well to do the same.

Now how do we do this? We read it. There is no substitute. You can read all sorts of books about the bible. There are a myriad of great teachers out there but those books are just God's revelation to them. He has a revelation prepared specifically for you. So let Him and his word abide in you (Jn. 15:7), meditate on the things found in God's word (Phil. 4:8) and renew your mind daily (Rom. 12:1-2)).

But don't just read it, heed it! Put into practice what you read (Phil. 4:9) and prove yourself a doer of the word and not just a hearer (James 2:15-17). Faith without works is dead faith. You may say you believe what you read but until you put it into practice you'll never know for sure.

And then repeat it. Take action. *"Proclaim the excellencies of him who has called you out of darkness into his marvelous light."* (1 Pet. 2:9) Then be ready in season and out of season to preach whenever you have the opportunity. (2 Tim. 4:2)

B.   PRAYER

Prayer is the discipline that I probably have the hardest time with. I don't really have a hard time talking to God but slowing down long enough to listen is pretty tough for me. I wrote about prayer pretty extensively in the third chapter, "Hearing from God," but let me just reiterate, that God sincerely wants to get in touch with you. His eyes *"move to and fro throughout the earth that he may strongly support those whose heart is completely his!"* (2 Chron. 16:9) He promises that if *"you will call upon me and come and pray to me…I will listen to you. And you will seek me and find me when you search for me with all your heart."* (Jer. 29:12-13) The problem isn't that God is hard to find. The problem is that most of us aren't looking.

After the fall in Genesis chapter 3 we see God walking through the garden searching for Adam and Eve even after they'd sinned, *"Where are you"* (3:9), he says. Of course God knew full well where they were and what they'd done but it reinforces the point that despite our mistakes he loves us and created us for fellowship with Him and eventually he would do whatever it took to restore that fellowship. But the ball's in our court. If we say that Jesus is our savior, provider, sustainer, redeemer, source of strength, life, light, and hope then what could be more important than getting to know him better each day. Talk to him. He's listening. And he's eager for a conversation. For more great books on prayer, take a look at Too Busy Not to Pray by Bill Hybels, Alone with God by John MacArthur and The Art of Prayer by Timothy Jones.

C.   FELLOWSHIP

It's also very important that we fellowship with like-minded believers. Not just church people but as Paul says, *"Those who call upon the Lord with a pure heart"* (2 Tim. 2:22) and there is a difference.

I received a letter from a friend recently who wrote, *"Matt, I need your help. I have been having an argument/discussion with someone about "going to church" and why I think it's important. He believes he is more religious than "church goers" as he can sit in his office and "converse with God." While I'm not denying he's a spiritual person, I just feel this is a "lazy excuse" for not going to church. I need some Biblical wisdom."*

This may surprise you but I'm not a real big fan of organized "church" or at least the way church has evolved in North America. I think our culture has so Americanized Jesus that the "church" today is more focused on our comfort and safety and living our best life now than with "going ye therefore."

Christianity is dirty. It's messy. Jesus ate with lepers and hung around prostitutes and sinners. He was not liked by the religious powers that be in his day. They called him a *"glutton and a wine bibber."* (Mt. 11:19) Jesus was not conservative. He was confrontational. He was provocative. He was definitely not safe! Following Christ today will likely lead you into uncomfortable and unsafe situations like the inner city, AIDS shelters, and corporate boardrooms. And while I realize I am painting with a broad brush I don't see that as the mission of far too many churches today. That having been said I don't believe it was ever meant for believers to worship in secret or in solitude. We need each other too much.

On the day of Pentecost Peter walked down from that upper room after being filled with the Holy Spirit and preached a whale of a sermon that led more than 3,000 people to the Lord. But he didn't do it alone. Acts 2:14 says he took *"his stand with the eleven!"* He was supported. He was encouraged. He was strengthened by their presence. In Acts 11:26 the early believers were strongly persecuted to the point of death yet they met once a week on the day that Jesus was resurrected (Sunday) and *"the disciples were first called Christians in Antioch."*

Since followers of Christ today are *"strangers and aliens"* (Eph. 2:19) to the rest of the world we still need the help and support of our brothers and sisters in Christ. We live according to a different standard. And living by that standard in this world demands that we worship together. Solomon wrote in Proverbs 17:17 that *"a friend loves at all time and a brother is born for adversity."* Tough times demand relationships.

He continued in Prov. 27:17 that *"Iron sharpens iron, so one man sharpens another."* In order for us to become the men and women we were created to be we need the accountability of a friend.

The writer of Hebrews knew that following Christ in a hostile world would not be easy so he extols his readers to *"hold fast the confession of our hope without wavering, for he who promised is faithful; and let US consider how to stimulate ONE ANOTHER to love and good deeds, not forsaking our own ASSEMBLING TOGETHER as is the habit of some but encouraging ONE ANOTHER and all the more as you see the day drawing near."* (Heb. 10:19-25)

Finally, the apostle Paul wrote to his son in the faith, Timothy, that in order to become the man he was created to be he had to *"flee youthful lusts, and pursue righteousness faith, love and peace WITH THOSE who call upon the Lord with a pure heart."* (2 Tim. 2:22)

The catch of it is, though, those people who call upon the Lord with a pure heart aren't always in your neighborhood church. (See Jude 1:4, 2 Tim. 4:2-4, Gal. 5:13-15, Phil. 2:1-15, 3:1-3, Col. 1:8, 18, 20-23 and on and on) We must be diligent to seek out followers of Christ who are not just dressing the part but actively *"pressing on toward the goal of the upward call of God in Christ Jesus."* (Phil. 3:14)

"Church" can take place in a coffee shop, on the golf course, in the office or out on the lake but it can't be alone. Fellowship with the Creator is wonderful and necessary but so are relationships with "the body."

D.   APPLYING YOUR GIFTS

Finally, a critical and maybe the most frightening aspect of discipline is applying the gifts, talents and abilities God has given you to furthering His kingdom. Now, while you may not think you possess anything special remember that while man looks at the outward appearance God sees your heart and your passion. And there are no insignificant roles in God's army.

Jonathan Ogden stands 6 feet 9 inches tall. And he weighs in at around 350 pounds. He is a mountain of a man who for more than a decade dominated defenders from the left side of the Baltimore Ravens offensive line. You don't want to mess with a guy like Jonathan Ogden. But Ogden didn't play much in 2007 because, well, he hurt his toe. That's right, this behemoth, this 10-time pro-bowler was unable to utilize his strong arms and powerful legs and enormous body because he hurt his big toe.

The docs call it 'Turf Toe' and it's no laughing matter. Turf toe actually ended the careers of Hall of Famers Deion Sanders and Jack Lambert among others. Go ahead and Google or Bing 'Turf Toe' for a detailed description of the injury and you'll see is it's a tough one from which to recover. And it should also remind us that in order for the body to operate as it's intended every joint, every muscle and every toe is important.

The Bible says that the body of Christ is held together *"by that which every joint supplies."* (Eph. 4:16) Recently our ministry was working to help a family rebuild a house that was blown apart by a storm. I saw a lot of joints on display that first weekend…I mean that in a legal way. There were old guys and college students. There were men and there were women. There were carpenters and there were laborers. And thank God there were cooks whose gifts of hospitality were much appreciated.

They were all there to help Gary and Donna Norwood provide a suitable home for their new family. It had been just about six months prior to this work weekend that Gary's brother in West Virginia passed away due to cancer at the age of 43. He left behind five kids, one of adult age but the others ranged in age from 17 to just 11. Though Gary's kids are grown and he thought he was done raising a family he did what brothers do and moved his nieces and his nephew into his house in Arkansas. His house in Arkansas, it should be noted, has only one bathroom and with three girls now under one roof, well, you get the idea.

So, one day, after his shift at the steel plant had ended, Gary began, all by himself, clearing the land for what he hoped would become a 1,900 square foot home. In his spare time, all by himself, Gary would lay the blocks then build the sub floor then frame in a wall, again, all by himself. His mail carrier, Donna Carter, watched the progress daily and when that storm came through and wiped away the months of hard work she had witnessed, well, she was heartbroken. She called a TV station to let them know. They left her on hold for too long. She then called my station. One of our reporters did the story. I read the story on the news the next day and something about it niggled at my spirit.

It didn't take much to sell my news director on the idea that helping the Norwood's finish the work Gary had started would be a good community service project. We contacted the local homebuilders association who put us in touch with contractor, Jim Childress, who agreed to serve as our quarterback. Then we put the word out over the airwaves and watched the good people of Arkansas respond. Have you noticed all the 'joints' in this story yet? We may not be able to do it alone but working together as a team anything's possible.

The body is indeed held together by that which every joint supplies and as each individual part works as it's supposed to the body is built up in love to the glory of God. As you might imagine, those kids that Gary and Donna took in have had a pretty rough life so far. What they witnessed over that weekend and in the subsequent month that followed was not cheap talk about how much God loves them but instead a real life, flesh and blood reflection of how Christ himself really feels about them. He loves them. He's especially fond of them and he wants them to live a fulfilling, abundant life as part of the body.

James says, *"Faith, if it has no works, is dead, being by itself."* (2:17) Apply your faith. It matters not whether you're Billy Graham or a big toe God put you here to make a difference and opportunities to make a difference aren't hard to find if you're looking.

RESOURCES

There are many other "spiritual disciplines," of course, and I encourage you to read up on them. Some good resources are <u>Celebration of Discipline</u> by Richard Foster, <u>Spiritual Disciplines for the Christian Life</u> by Donald Whitney, and <u>Spirit of the Disciplines</u> by Dallas Willard. That ought to be enough to get you started!

Chapter Six

Passion

"Hang in there. Keep on a going. Today we're going to succeed!"
-Atocha Captain, Mel Fisher

"And immediately he made the disciples get into the boat, and go ahead of Him to the other side, while He sent the multitudes away." (Mt. 14:22)

He *made* the disciples get into the boat. Did that word stand out to you, too? You know, the Bible's kind of funny like that. No matter what you're reading somehow God's word can reach you right where you are. The writer of Hebrews says, ***"The word of God is living and active and sharper than a two-edged sword."*** (4:12) I think that's why you can sometimes read the same verse on different days and it will say something totally different to you.

Maybe the reason that word "made" speaks so loudly to me is because I'm a guy and it says to me that perhaps, despite what I was led to believe as a kid, Jesus was a guy, too. See, I grew up in the church, a bunch of churches really; Presbyterian, Bible, Wesleyan, Methodist, Baptist and so on. We moved a lot. But no matter what church I found myself in the pattern was pretty much the same. All of my Sunday school teachers were women. All of my Vacation Bible School teachers were women. When I went to children's church: women. So the image I was given of Jesus was filtered through the eyes of the ladies, nothing wrong with that. In fact, thank God for godly women without whom there wouldn't be too many men in Heaven. I mean how many of us starting going to church in the first place because of women, first our moms and then to meet that cute girl. Be honest.

Still, the image that I had of Jesus growing up was the image that many of these ladies identified with. When they read through the scriptures they saw a kind, sweet, loving, tender, caring, compassionate, long-haired, green-eyed hippy. And that's the image they presented to me. And apparently a lot of us had the same Sunday school teacher because in just about every church I visit I see that picture of Jesus with the long blond hair, Roman nose, green eyes kneeling in the garden looking ever so effeminately off into the distance…you know the one.

But when I got to college and started reading the Bible as opposed to having it read to me, I got a totally different picture of who Jesus was. Or at least I got another side of him. Yeah, Jesus was kind, sweet, tender, loving, caring and compassionate. But you know what? He was also a man. In fact he was kind of a man's man. I mean He was a carpenter before Black & Decker. He had power tools hanging from his shoulders. Jesus was not just this kind, sweet guy. He was the kind of guy that makes disciples go where they don't want to go. And they didn't want to get into the boat. They wanted to help him send the multitudes away. They weren't a lot of help with that multitude in the first place so they figured they'd make up for it now but Jesus says, *"Get into the boat. I've got something to show you. I've got something to teach you. I want you in the boat right now."*

And the disciples say, *"Yeah, but Jesus…"*
"Get in the boat," He says.

"But Jesus we want to help you…"
"Do ya feel lucky? Well, do ya, punks?" (My apologies to Clint Eastwood.)

He 'makes' them get into the boat the same way he 'puts out' the professional mourners when Jairus' daughter dies. (Mk. 5:41) The same way he starts flipping over tables in the temple when he sees people standing between God and his children trying to get to God. (Jn. 2:15) That's the kind of man Jesus was. He wasn't a macho man. He was a righteous man. He stood in the gap. He fought for the little guy. He got things done. Guys, read the Bible. Don't just have it read to you. Read this thing because God has got something to show you. He might even show in one little word.

Anyway, back to the boat. The Bible says after the disciples got into the boat Jesus sent them on ahead of him to the other side while he sent the multitudes away. *"After he sent the multitude away he went to the mountain by himself to pray."* (Mt. 14:23) See, there's another indication that Jesus was a manly man. When he wanted to get together with his father, where did he go? To the deer woods, that's right!

Sorry…He went up by himself to the mountains to pray, *"But the boat was already far from the land, battered by the waves for the wind was contrary. In the fourth watch of the night,"* about three to six o'clock in the morning, *"he came to them walking on the sea. When the disciples saw him walking on the sea they were frightened."* They were afraid and they said, *"It is a ghost,"* and they cried out for fear. *"But immediately Jesus spoke to them and said, 'Take courage. It is I. Do not be afraid.'"* (Mt. 14:24-27) Boy, that is a *big* statement right there. In the original language it goes something like: *Be bold. I AM. Fear not.* In other words, "Be courageous. I am the Lord. Don't be afraid." Folks, we've got to put those words over our door before we walk out of the house. Those are words to live by.

And look at what Peter says when he hears those powerful words, *"Lord, if it is You, command me to come to You on the water!"* (28) Think about that for a moment. Is that not about the stupidest thing you've ever heard in your life? I mean it's in the Bible so we'll cut him some slack but honestly does Peter really think that he can walk on water? The guy's a fisherman. He's been on this water his whole life. He knows that if you step out of a perfectly good boat you're going to sink or swim…not walk. So why on earth would he say such a thing? Well, in his video series, <u>In The Dust of the Rabbi</u>, historian and author Ray Vander Laan helped me understand a little bit more about the times in which the disciples lived.

The Bible tells us that the religious people of the day called the disciples *"uneducated and untrained men."* (Acts 4:13) And some of us have come to believe that what that means is that the disciples were an ignorant bunch of yahoos. But what that phrase really meant was that these guys didn't go to rabbinical school. In the west we'd say they didn't go to seminary. They weren't stupid because as Vander Laan explains it was very important in this culture that all Hebrew children, including the girls, know how to read and write. For the kids who grew up in Bethsaida and Capernaum including Peter, Andrew, James, John and Phillip they would go to school at the synagogue in Chorazin. That school was known as Beth Sefer. There the Rabbi or the Rabbi's assistant would teach the kids how to read and write by reading the Torah or what we know as the first five books of the Bible written by Moses; Genesis, Exodus, Leviticus, Numbers and Deuteronomy.

They would read and write what they learned from these books over and over until they knew the history and the law of the Hebrew people backwards and forward and they did this until they were about twelve years old. And when they got to that age most all of the kids would go back to their families and learn the family business. But there was a small group of kids who didn't want to leave school. They liked this stuff. They wanted to learn more. So instead of going fishing or making tables they went to another school called Beth Midrash. Here they would study the prophets and the psalms and take their education to a whole new level. And when they would get to be about 19 or 20 years old they, too, would go back into society.

But again there were those kids, a very small, select, elite group of kids that said, "I want more!" So they would go to the Rabbi and say, "Rabbi, I want to follow you," and they would follow the rabbi wherever he went and they would listen to him teach. They would see what he saw. They would experience what he experienced. For a time there they were his shadow. In fact there was an old Hebrew saying that these students wanted *"to be covered in the dust of the rabbi's feet."* They would follow him so closely that the dust from his steps was all over them. But

62

they didn't just want to learn from the rabbi they wanted to be who the rabbi was and to absorb as much of his essence as they could so they followed him everywhere. And these students were known as the *Talmid* or disciples.

And it's in this environment, in this culture, Vander Laan says, that we hear Peter say what he said. Remember Peter's education. See, he knew *exactly* what Jesus meant when he said, "I AM," because he'd memorized Exodus. He remembered when Moses went before God and said, "What is your name?" and God responded, *"I AM WHO I AM."* (Ex. 3:14) Jesus used the same word God did to describe Himself. Peter heard that and responds to the call to be bold, *"Lord, if it is you...if you are really who you say you are, you tell me to get out of this boat and I'll come out there to you."*

No, it didn't make any sense. He's in the middle of a storm. Stepping out of a boat is nuts...but the rabbi is out there in the deep water calling to him and as a disciple, as a follower of Christ, there's no place on earth he'd rather be even if it means risking his own life.

The first element in being a follower of Jesus Christ is passion.

OBSESSION

In order to be a disciple you have to *want* to be a disciple. Proverbs 4:7 says, *"The beginning of wisdom is: Acquire wisdom."* In other words if you want to be wise you have to *want* to be wise. You have to seek after it. It must be your desire, your passion. Do you desire Christ? Do you want to be where Jesus is? Peter had to get out there in the deep water whether it made any sense to anybody or not. Is that how you see your relationship with Christ? Is following after him your obsession?

You know, most radio or television reporters have their favorite interviews. Let me tell you about one of mine. His name is Mel Fisher and to tell his story I have to go all the way back to 1622. That was the year that the Spanish galleon, Atocha, was being loaded down in Havana with large trunks containing gold and silver bars, emeralds, rubies, coins, and other treasures bound for Spain. But just two days after setting sail the Atocha and the rest of her flotilla was destroyed by a hurricane. Spanish officials marked the wreckage but were unable to retrieve it. Sixty days later a second hurricane came through and the Atocha vanished without a trace.

Three hundred and fifty years later this guy, Mel Fisher, believed he knew where the Atocha lay. So he gathered the crew and raised the money and began his quest to find the sunken treasure. Beginning in 1969 Mel said he would wake up his crew with the words, *"Hang in there and keep on a-going. Today we're going to succeed!"* In 1973 they found three silver bars. Two years later five bronze cannons from the Atocha were uncovered but still no treasure. Yet, every morning, *"Hang in there and keep on a going. Today we're going to succeed!"*

I wondered what could keep a man going despite years of failure. Mel said he just knew the treasure existed. He knew it had to be there. So year after year he convinced investors to back him and year after year he kept searching, kept digging, kept diving and kept coming up empty. Then on the morning of July 20, 1985, sixteen years after he began his quest, Mel received this message from his son, *"Put away the charts; we've found the Mother lode!"* Within days divers began retrieving what amounted to 47 tons of silver, 150,000 gold coins and bars and millions of dollars in precious gems.

Have you ever wanted something so badly it became on obsession? Finding the Atocha was Mel Fisher's obsession. He would not be deterred by naysayers. He pursued his obsession with the determination of a cheetah in search of a gazelle. He asked and kept on asking. He knocked and kept on knocking. He sought and kept on seeking. And like the woman of Luke 18 his persistence, his obsession was rewarded.

What's your obsession? What's your passion? What are you seeking after? Is it working? Has it satisfied or do you keep grasping for more? Ever heard of a guy named Tom Brady? Of course you have. Tom

Brady is the quarterback of the 3-time Super Bowl champion New England Patriots. He's rich, famous, handsome and let's face it…he's a chick magnet. Most guys want to be just like Tom Brady and most girls want you to be just like him as well! Anyway, Tom Brady recently told 60 Minutes a few years back, *"Why do I have 3 Super Bowl rings and still think there's something greater out there for me? I reached my goal, my dream, my life…I think, God, it's got to be more than this. I mean this…can't be what it's all cracked up to be!"* (CBS News 60 Minutes 11/6/05)

Long before Tom Brady came to be, King Solomon was Tom Brady; fame, money, power and you talk about chicks! He had every carnal desire satisfied and yet he writes in Eccl. 2:17, ***"The work which I had been done under the sun was grievous to me; because everything is futility and striving after the wind."***

Trying to find an abundant, contented and purpose-filled life on our own terms just won't work. The Lord told the prophet Jeremiah, ***"My people have committed two evils; they've forsaken me the river of living water to dig for themselves cisterns, broken cisterns that can hold no water."*** (Jer. 2:13)

Only by following after Christ will you find the life you're searching for. Psalm 139:15 says that God made you in secret; just you and Him. He knows how and why you were put together. Heb. 12:1 says God has set before you a race that only you can run. There's a purpose for you being here. And in Matt. 6:33 Jesus says if you seek after him first and his righteousness he'll take care of everything else you need.

What are you pursuing to find the life your heart desires? If it's anything other than Christ you'll end up with a cheap imitation of the abundant life he created you to live

Pursue Christ. Pursue him like a cheetah after a gazelle. Pursue him like that guy who found a treasure and hides it in a field, ***"And from joy over*** *it he goes and sells all that he has and buys the field."* (Mt. 13:44) Or like that merchant seeking after fine pearls who, *"Upon finding one pearl of great value he went and sold all that he had and he bought it."*

Can't you feel the passion those two guys had when they found that treasure? Is that how we feel about the kingdom? See, I'm afraid unless we make Christ the center of our existence, the hub around which everything else rotates that we'll never become the people he created us to be.

"But, Matt, I don't have that passion. I don't have that fire. I don't have that obsession to serve God." I had a friend who told me that once. So I asked him, *"What is your passion? What is your focus?"* He said, *"Man, I haven't got one. I don't know what God wants me to do with my life. I don't really have a passion – a driving desire."*

So we hung around together. We talked. We ate. We worked. I encouraged. I mentored – and he started reading God's word. He started having prayer time with God. He started going to a Bible study and fellowshipping daily with others who were also pursuing Christ. The next thing you know God starts blessing this guy up one side and down the other. He ignites a passion that had been buried under years of trying to do for himself. Now my friend tells me, *"I just want to serve God no matter how he wants me to serve him. Here I am God. Send me."*

Yeah, passion can be stoked. But it's up to you. Some of you had the passion a long time ago but you dismissed it. You ignored it. You let it die down. Well, like Paul tells Timothy, it's time to stir it up. You, and only you, have to *"kindle afresh the gift of God which is in you."* (2 Tim. 1:6) Again, God says in 2 Chronicles 16:9 that he's just waiting to strongly support you if you'll give Him your whole heart. But the choice is yours.

We can inspire. We can encourage. We can motivate and we can stimulate others to stir up the gift. But the key is, if you're having trouble figuring out where that passion is, where that fire is, you've got to look in the mirror and make a choice. Humble yourself before God and don't conform to this world, but transform yourself through the renewing of your mind. Grow in favor with God and you'll be able to prove what the will of God is for your life, that which is good and acceptable and perfect. (Rom. 12:1-2) The closer you draw to the shepherd, the more clearly you're able to distinguish his voice (Jn. 10:27) and the more that passion will begin to consume you.

But passion is only the first step.

Chapter Seven

Courage

"Your heart is free. Have the courage to follow it!"
-Braveheart

I have a very good friend who lives about 45 minutes away from me. Anytime I find myself close to his town I make it a point to pay him a visit. I just love spending time with the guy. He's one of those friends who even if you haven't seen each other for weeks the minute you sit down with him it's like you haven't been apart at all.

One day while I sat in his office and the small talk was winding to a close he looked me dead in the eyes and told me he felt God was calling him to be a worship leader. I wasn't surprised. This wasn't the first time he'd mentioned that God was pulling him in that direction. I mean the dude can sing and so can his wife. And you ought to hear that woman play the piano!

But I could tell there was more to the story this time so I gave him some room. He said, *"I just really feel like God wants me to lead worship somewhere, some how, some way. So the other night (my wife) and I prayed about it. A week later I get a phone call from this pastor of a pretty big church here in town. I've never met the man but he said he'd heard about me from a mutual friend and he wanted me and (my wife) to lead worship for their revival!"*

"That's awesome!" I said. *"What a confirmation! You prayed and God answered your prayer just like that. When's the revival?"*

"Uh, I said no."

"You did what? Why?"

"I don't know. I...I just couldn't do it. I was too afraid."

To this day every time I visit that guy he still tells me he feels God wants him leading worship. But it's one thing to say, *"Jesus tell me to get out of this boat and I'll walk out there to you."* It's quite another to obey him when he says, *"Alright...come here!"*

See, my friend has the passion. He has the fire. He has the desire. But when he stares over the edge of that boat all he sees are the waves and he just can't make himself let go. And when you think about it not much has changed in the past 2000 years.

Put yourself back out there on the boat with Peter. The rain's falling. The waves are rolling. The boat's being tossed to and fro. You see what appears to be a ghost walking out to you on the water. All of the sudden that ghost shouts above the waves, ***"Take courage, I AM, don't be afraid!"*** For a minute you can't believe your ears. *"Did he say I AM? Is that...Jesus? Lord, if it is you, if you are who you say you are just say the word and I'll come out there on the water to you!"*

And then he says, *"Come!"*

"Uh...you mean, like, now, in front of all these people? What if I don't make it? What if I look like a fool? What if I fail? I want to come out there to you but...yikes!

You wouldn't be alone with those thoughts. That why Jesus put those disciples in that boat in the first place. Take a look at Mark 6:47 and 48. It's the same story from Matthew 14 it's just told from a different perspective. See Matthew was written by...Matthew and Mark by a guy names John Mark. But unlike Matthew Mark wasn't one of the twelve. So where did he get his information? Peter. Mark was sort of like Peter's biographer. Peter was telling the stories and Mark was writing them down. And while Mark omits the part about Peter walking on the water, he does include a little snippet about the occasion that Matthew doesn't…and it's a pretty big snippet.

Mark writes, *"Seeing them straining at the oars, for the wind was against them, at about the fourth watch of the night, He came to them, walking on the sea: and he intended to pass them by."* (48)

Hmmm. So just like in Matthew we read there's a big storm that comes up while the disciples are in the boat. The wind is whipping, the waves are crashing, and the boys are afraid for their lives. Jesus sees them and knows they're in trouble. He knows this is a situation with which he needs to get involved. So he begins to walk on the water out there to help them but as Mark says, *"he intended to pass them by."*

Now does that make any sense to you? Why in the world would Jesus go through the trouble of walking on top of the white caps if he's just going to walk right on by? Do you ever feel like God does that to you? I mean, you've got a major league problem in your life. It's a soul stirring dilemma, one that may cost you everything you have. You lift up your prayers and petitions before him to help you. You pray specifically for the problem and tell God in no uncertain terms what He needs to do about it. And the answer you receive in return is the exact opposite of what you wanted God to do.

Its crazy isn't it. But remember, at least half of these disciples grew up on this water. They'd sailed across this sea hundreds of times if not more. So when Jesus calls them to go to the other side most of them figured they knew exactly how to accomplish His will. So they jockey for position inside the boat, put together a mission statement and a five year plan then send out a fund-raising letter. And that's about the time that the wind picked up. And despite all of their wisdom, knowledge, experience, strength and ability their boat went nowhere. All they could do was *"strain at the oars."* They knew how to get from one side of the sea to the other but they just weren't able to do it their way.

70

There's a reason for the storms in your life. It's the same reason Jesus allowed the wind and the waves to come against the disciples. See, one day very soon those boys crying out there in that boat would become the leaders of the first century church. They were going to have to believe beyond a shadow of a doubt that Jesus was indeed the Christ. Nearly all would be asked to give their very lives in order to advance the kingdom. But at this point they were far from ready. They needed to grow. They needed to be challenged. They needed to be stretched beyond what they believed. So at the height of their fear Jesus comes out there to them…but he's not coming to their boat. They weren't going to accomplish His will their way. If they wanted to become the men God created them to be they were going to have to suspend what they knew, step out of that boat, and follow him in faith to the other side.

Now, did you notice that only one guy, only one in twelve, less than 10% of those who heard the call, actually obeyed? Again, things haven't changed much in 2000 years. See, it takes more than passion to follow God. It takes courage. Why? Because following after Christ is crazy. It's nuts. God's will for your life is not going to make any sense to you or anyone else around you. In fact most of your well meaning friends and family will try to talk you out of following Christ out of the boat. And that's just the way He wants it.

Seriously, think about it, if you could accomplish in your wisdom, knowledge and ability what God has called you to do who would get the glory? That's why God's going to ask you to do things that are *way* beyond your ability so that you're forced to get your faith and trust off of you and on to Him because in order for you to do what he has called you to do and live that overpowering, overcoming, abundant life that he has called you to live, you can't do it your way – and he knows that. God says in Jeremiah 2:13, *"My people have committed two evils: They have forsaken Me, the fountain of living waters, the hew for themselves cisterns, broken cisterns that can hold no water."* In other words, you can try to attain the abundant life on your own terms but you'll only end up with a very cheap, unsatisfactory imitation. So with your best interests in mind He's going to challenge you just like he challenged some of his other children…like Abraham.

ABRAHAM-Genesis 12

"Abraham, I want you to pack up everything you have and I want you to follow me into an unknown direction." So Abraham packs up everything he has; all of his sheep, goats, tents, everything and says to God, *"Alright God, I'm all packed up. Now where are we going?"*

And God says, *"None of your business. I'll tell you when we get there."*

Now can you follow God when you don't know where he's leading you? Can you follow God when he hasn't really told you specifically where you are going? Can you follow him in that situation? Brother, that takes courage. How about Gideon?

GIDEON-Judges 7 & 8

God told Gideon, *"Go fight the Midianites. I have delivered them into your hand."* Now, Gideon knew that there were about 135,000 Midianites. Still he says, *"You got it, God. I've got 30-some thousand screaming soldiers. We can do it. I know we're outmatched, but if you brought them into our hands, we'll do it."*

And God says, *"You've got 30,000 soldiers? And they've got 135,000? Dude, YOU'VE got too many."* And when you read the story in Judges 6 and 7, you see that God whittled Gideon's army down to what? Three hundred men…against 135,000! Now, can you follow God when it looks like defeat is certain? Can you follow God when what he's asking you to do is going to lead to your humiliation? Can you follow God in that situation? Take a look at Noah.

NOAH-Genesis 6 & 7

"I want you to build me an ark, Noah, a great big one, big enough to hold all the critters on the planet, two by two. Because I'm going to make it rain for 40 days and 40 nights."

Of course, Noah's first question was probably, *"What's rain?"* As far as I can tell from the scriptures up to that point it had never rained. I should know…I'm a meteorologist! The Bible says in Genesis 2:6 that God was watering the earth from the ground. But as soon as God explained rain to Noah I'm sure his next question was, *"What's an ark?"* I mean, Noah lived hundreds of miles away from the nearest large body of water. That's why God was so specific with those instructions and dimensions.

And of course as if none of that was crazy enough look at the man's age! The Bible says Noah was 500 years old when he started to pound that thing together. *Five hundred years old!* (Gen. 5:32) And he was 600 years old when the flood came. (Gen. 7:6) Do the math! That means that boat sat in Noah's front yard up on blocks for 100 years! You realize that makes Noah the world's first redneck, don't you? I mean he's got a boat in the front yard up on blocks…couple of coon dogs underneath the front porch, but only two of them, male and female. Can't you see the people coming from all over the countryside laughing at poor old Noah? Can you imagine what his neighbors were saying about him?

Now, do you have the courage to follow God when what he's asking you to do is going to make you look like a fool? Are you ready to follow at the expense of your power, position and popularity? It takes a tremendous amount of courage to step out of that boat when everyone in your church, your family and your circle of friends is telling you that you're crazy if you do. But I'm here to tell you it will cost you even more if you don't. Because until you take that chance you'll never really know for sure that God is who he says he is and will do what he's promised he will do.

Let me close out this chapter with a quick story of how I learned that lesson first hand. It started with a concrete slab.

MIRACLE AT MT. LAKE

The 4,000 square foot slab had been poured right next to the Mt. Lake Missionary Baptist Church; a rickety old building with a steeple that was leaning hard to one side and paint that at one time must have been pretty. I remember thinking when I first saw it that it was about time they built a new church. A good gust of wind was surely going to take care of the old one any day now. When I noticed the slab again the following year I just figured they were still raising money. But by the third year I knew something was wrong. And that's about the time I heard God's voice.

Earlier that year I had been asked to help lead music at the First Baptist Church of England, Arkansas. I didn't want to lead the music. I told them that. Twice. I'm not the music minister type. I'm not a good organizer. I can't read music. I can sing but that doesn't qualify me to lead a choir. Besides, music ministers work too hard. But the music committee was very nice and took me out to lunch so as a way to dismiss them without losing face I told them I'd pray about it. And no matter how hard I tried I couldn't get God to say, "No!"

So, stepping out of my boat, in December of 2002, I became the 'part-time, interim minister of music' at the First Baptist Church of England. No, I didn't miraculously turn into a good music man but I did get to drive by that slab two or three times a week. And it was during the summer of 2003 on my way to a Sunday morning service that I heard God tell me in a voice as clear as if He was sitting next to me, *"I want you to build a church on that slab."*

"Build? Me? God you've seen me build and you know I don't have any money." He wasn't impressed.

I tried to rationalize what I'd heard. Was that really God telling me that? Then a couple of weeks later my friend Dave Perry and his wife Kay came down to England to hear me sing. After the service we engaged in a little small talk then out of the blue David asks me, *"You know that little white church on the highway?"*

"Uh...yeah," I stammered.

"I've just felt a burden to do something for that church." Bam! There you go. ***"By the mouth of two or three witnesses every fact may be confirmed."*** (Matt. 18:16)

Two Sundays later, after our service was over, I headed down the highway and nervously knocked on the door of the Mt. Lake Missionary Baptist Church and learned that black folks worship a whole lot longer than white folks. It was nearly 12:30 and they were still singing. But let me tell you, when that door opened and the congregation got a look at my blonde hair and blue eyes...the singing stopped! But I was graciously received by one of the deacons and when he inquired as to the purpose of my visit I looked that good man right in the eyes and said without a hint of fear, *"I believe God wants me to help you build a church. Would that be OK?"*

I discovered later that deacon, whose name was Londell White, had recognized me from television and assumed I was loaded and was going to pay for all the repairs myself. He couldn't help hide the disappointment when I explained to him in my living room a few days later that I was broke and was trusting God for all of our provisions. Though I'm sure he felt he was wasting his time he handed over his architectural plans anyway and I immediately handed them over to my friend Jerry.

I'd known of Jerry Thompson from church but didn't really know him until I was asked to go on a mission trip to Illinois earlier that summer. We went there to tear down an old building for a ministry that was planning on building a new one in its place later that year. Jerry, as it turned out, was a building contractor in North Little Rock. He built houses. He was also pretty good at tearing them down. I also learned that Jerry went on several foreign mission trips a year to build schools, churches and other buildings. One night as we sat recuperating from our destructive work, I told Jerry about this little white church on highway 165. I wondered would it be possible for us to gather enough men and money to at least build them a shell of a building. Knowing he was being talked into another charity project, Jerry gave me a cautious yes. I believe God sent me on that mission trip just so I could meet Jerry.

Anyway, Jerry took the plans and developed a materials list along with a price list. David and I then prayed about when we should begin and each came up with the date of Nov. 7th-9th which was really kind of stupid. See, Nov. 7th-9th of that year was the start of modern gun deer season which is kind of a big deal in Arkansas. Seriously, it wasn't too long ago that schools would let out for a week at the opening of deer season. Still, that's the date God gave us so that's the date we choose.

As November 7th drew near Jerry informed me that if we planned to build on that date we needed to order the trusses for the roof and we needed to order them at least 3 weeks prior to building. I said sure, fine...what's a truss? Once he explained to me they were the triangular foundations of the roof I inquired as to where one might find a truss? He pointed me toward a local company that made them so with plans in hand I paid them a visit to put in my order.

The folks at River City Truss couldn't have been nicer. I told them a little about the mission project, showed them the plans then waited for the bottom line. *"Well, tell you what,"* the man said, *"Since this is a ministry deal, we'll let you have the trusses for...$5,300. How's that sound?"*

Now at the time I had about, oh, $300 in my ministry account. So here I was on the edge of fact and faith. Did I really believe that God had called me to this project? And if so, did I really believe that He would supply my needs according to his riches in glory? (Phil. 4:19) I did. So against all common sense and fiscal responsibility I stuck out my hand and said, "Let's do it!"

No kidding, a few days later the England newspaper ran a small story about the project. Shortly after that I received a call from an evangelist in town named Charles Capps who said, *"God's been telling me to do something for that church for months now but every time I drive by no one's there. When I saw the story in the newspaper I guessed that was my burning bush. So I'm sending you a check for $5,000. I hope it helps."* Uh, yeah, Charles, it helped, in more ways than one!

So, we had our trusses. Of course we had nothing upon which to place them but we had our trusses. It would take another $7,000 to buy the rest of the phase one materials. So I paid a visit to every rich person I knew. Not one of them gave me a dime. It wasn't that these weren't giving people. They were. Most of them cheerfully glorified God with their money. But in this case God chose not to use those wealthy individuals. Instead like Moses getting water from a rock God chose to bless us in ways that truly brought Him the glory; $100 from Coy, $250 from Stuttgart, a $10 check from a sweet lady in Almyra, and a $1,000 check from a couple in England just for starters.

One afternoon, as we were nailing deck boards to the roof, I told David that we needed about $3,000 to get us in the clear. An hour or so later we were eating lunch at a great little restaurant in nearby Keo called Charlotte's Eats and Sweets when an elderly man slowly escorted his wife to our table. They were dressed rather modestly, he in overalls and she in a simple dress. Neither moved with any sort of fluency and there was nothing about them that would indicate wealth of any kind. Still they lit up the room when the walked in. The man said he and his wife had seen a story about our project on television and she was touched by our efforts and wanted to help. With hands that were shaking from age she wrote out a check for $3,000. David wept.

I could go on and on with these kinds of stories of God's provision. One man donated the cabinets and countertops. Another man installed a sound system. One day we found a note on the church door asking us to visit a Little Rock contractor named Bill Clark. When we shared with him that we had nearly everything done except for the insulation, drywall and floor treatment. He looked at us and said, *"I'll take care of that."* He provided the materials and the labor which we estimated cost about $40,000!

Our initial goal was to build the walls, shingle the roof and if we had enough money to put in windows and doors. We figured Mt. Lake could handle the rest. But God had other plans. While we worked, people literally drove by and dropped off checks and donated services. Five months after the opening day of deer season on that drizzly November morning we handed to the leadership of Mt. Lake Missionary Baptist Church the keys to a brand new 4000 square foot worship center without one cent of debt.

You know, you can say all day that *"I can do all things through Him who strengthens me"* (Phil. 4:13) or *"My God shall supply all your needs according to His riches in glory"* (Phil. 4:19) but unless you have the courage to step out of the boat and put your faith to the test you'll never really know for sure. In mentoring his son in the faith, Timothy, the apostle Paul wrote, *"I know whom I have believed and I'm convinced that he is able to guard what I have entrusted to Him until that day."* (2 Tim. 1:12) How did Paul know that? What was the reason for his confidence? Simple, he kept putting God's word to the test. He kept stepping further and further out of the boat. He kept pressing on toward the upward call and God was always there. (Phil. 3:8-14) If God calls you he will also enable you to do the impossible.

But now let me warn you and I'm just keeping it real, here. There is a very good chance that when you step out of that boat for the first time you're going to fail. But that's OK. Since my journey over the edge I've made it a point to ask others out there in the deep water about their journey and just about everyone I've met has failed in one way or the other. Nothing they tried worked. And many had lost everything they had and to a person they would tell you – it was the best thing that ever happened to them.

It was the best thing that ever happened to me. I lost everything I had. But when I was down to nothing and had no wisdom, knowledge or ability to make this ministry work, that's when God said, *"Good. Now I've got you where I want you. Now you're going to have to rely upon me and my power and provision."*
And like a Marine drill sergeant who takes a raw recruit and disabuses him of 20 years of thinking for himself in order to build him up as part of a team, God began to transform me into the man I was created to be.

Yeah, when you step out over the edge you might fail. Peter did. He stepped out and within a few steps he began to sink. But was that really a failure? Did Jesus make a mistake asking him to step out? Nah. That very same Peter who once cried out for Jesus to save him from drowning also wrote years later that God uses that failure; he uses those trials to personally *"perfect, confirm, strengthen and establish you."* (I Pet. 5:10) So go on. Take the shot!

Chapter Eight

Faith

"Go the Distance."
- Field of Dreams

Again, I've shared with you my background of how I grew up in the church. I had a Bible with my name engraved on it for as long as I can remember. I think I even got a gift certificate once for memorizing all the books of the Bible in order. Of course I memorized them in a song.

"Matthew, Mark, Luke, John, Acts and the epistle to the Romans
First, Second Corinthians, Galatians and Ephesians..."

Anyway, I've always had a Bible I just haven't always read it. I didn't really start doing that until I got to college, believe it or not. See, there was this girl...it's a long story. The point is I discovered that when you read the word as opposed to having it read to you, you discover some pretty cool things such as the word of God is constantly changing. Easy now...I know some of you just blew a gasket. What I mean is I know God is the same yesterday, today and forever...but I'm not. One day I'm a boy without a care in the world, the next day I have a zit on my chin before my first big date! A week later I'm taking college finals and getting married and having babies and losing my hair! And God's word is right there with me seamlessly adapting to every change in my life. Yeah, the words may be the same but their relevance and impact grows as I do.

For example, this verse: ***"But seeing the wind he became afraid and he began to cry out, 'Lord, save me.' And immediately Jesus stretched out his hand and took hold of him and said to him, 'Oh you of little faith, why did you doubt?'"***

Now, I always thought when Jesus said, *"Oh you of little faith, why did you doubt"* that he meant, *"Peter, why did you lose faith in me? Don't you still believe that I'm the Messiah, that I'm God, and that I can enable you to do what I have commanded you to do? Why did you lose faith in me?"* I always thought that's what he meant.

Then one day I looked at the story again and I noticed something. Where was Jesus when he asked Peter that question? On top of the water, right? Where was Peter? He was going *"glub, glub."* Peter never lost faith that Jesus was the Messiah. He never lost faith that Jesus was God. Jesus is still standing on top of the sea while he's doing his best not to drink it all! So in whom did Peter lose faith? That's right...himself!

Wow, that just sounds so...unbiblical, doesn't it? Have faith in yourself? Isn't that's the problem? Isn't our heart desperately wicked? Isn't our lust of the eyes, lust of the flesh and sinful pride of life how we got into this mess in the first place? Shouldn't we just have faith in God and not ourselves? Well, you know what in order to be a disciple you're going to need a little of both. Let me explain.

THE CLOSER YOU GET

Remember one of the first times that we see Peter and Jesus together? Take a look at Luke chapter 5. There's a great story where Jesus is preaching along the shore of the Sea of Galilee and people are coming from all over the countryside to hear him. The people soon begin to crowd in on him and push him back toward the water. He's getting closer and closer to the shore and before long he finds himself standing in the water and his robe is beginning to get wet, you know that white robe with the blue sash, yeah that one. About that time he spots some men who've been fishing all night. They were cleaning the nets even though after all that work they hadn't caught anything. And he says to them, *"Hey boys can I borrow your boat?"*

He then goes on to preach a whale of a sermon and when it was over he asks Peter to take him fishing. Now, Peter, who was already mad, tired and hungry and just wanted to get to bed could hardly disguise his frustration, *"You know, Lord, we fished pretty hard...all night...and didn't catch a thing. But if that's what you want..."* and he heads out to the deep water. After several minutes of sailing, Jesus, the carpenter, lets Peter, the professional fisherman, know he'd found a good spot to let down the nets. So as Peter clenched his teeth and muttered a few choice words under his breath he threw out his freshly cleaned nets...right on top of the mother lode!

The next thing you know fish are coming out of everywhere, filling up the nets so full that they begin to tear. Peter hollers for his partners, most likely James, John and Zebedee. They begin to fill their boats so full of fish that they begin to sink. And there's Jesus with this big 'ole grin on his face watching it all happen. I've always wondered if this was just Jesus' way of thanking Peter for letting him borrow his boat. Remember fishing was how Peter made a living and he hadn't caught a thing the night before. A couple of boats full of fish would go a long way to paying off some bills.

Or maybe it was because of what Peter did next. As he watched his crews fill up the boats with fish he began to realize something amazing was happening, something...miraculous? He'd been fishing all of his life and never had he heard of anything like this. Then he looks at Jesus. He'd heard him teach. He'd watched him heal. Could he be...the One? And he falls on his face and says, **"Depart from me, for I am a sinful man, O Lord."** (Luke 5:8)

You know, I've felt like that before. It happened several years ago. I haven't always been as good looking as I am today. There was a time when I was bit...chunkier. But I went on a diet, began to work out again and had lost a bunch of weight. I took my family to mom and dad's house for Christmas and I was anxious to show off my new physique. We walked in and they couldn't stop fussing over me. "You look so skinny!" "How'd you do it?" "Where'd your butt go?" It was great and

I was feeling pretty fine. Then my brother walked in…my Army Ranger brother. He'd been overseas for a while and got home just in time for the holidays. Now, I love my brother more than ice cream and was happy he was home but as I went to hug him something amazing happened. The closer I got to his six-foot, muscle-bound frame the fatter I became. The closer I got to physical perfection the greater my physical flaws appeared.

And that's exactly what happens to Peter in that fishing boat…and out there in that deep water.

NOT ME, LORD

God personally calls him out of his boat and he steps over the edge and begins to walk on water. Yeah, really! He's walking on top of the water! Can you imagine what he's thinking? *"Dude, this is so cool. I'm walking on water. This is awesome. Nobody in the history of the world has ever walked on water. Look at me."* And then all of the sudden it hit him – *"You know nobody in the history of the world has ever walked on water."*

And as he looks into the eyes of Jesus he begins to think, *"Lord, I have no business being out here. I mean you; you're God, but me? You don't know the things that I think or the things that I've done. You don't know the kind of person I am. Do you know what I did last week or last year or was thinking about doing tomorrow? You've called the wrong guy, Jesus. You need to call some holy guy to do what you've created me to do, not me. I am not worthy to be out here on the same body of water as you."* And all of the sudden his guilt and shame and his past come flooding down upon him along with all that sea water.

HONOR STUDENTS

Ever felt that way? Guilt and shame are powerful shackles. I think it's probably helpful now that I finish my story about the Talmid from chapter 6. Remember the Talmid were the brightest of the bright. They were the valedictorians of rabbinical school. After everyone else went back into the world to work, the Talmid wanted to learn more. So they would approach the rabbi and boldly say, *"I want to follow you!"* And if they were good enough the rabbi would allow it. And this was the way it was for centuries. The honor students would ask the rabbi if they were good enough to follow him. Then along comes the rabbi...Jesus.

Never one for convention, Jesus turned the age-old practice on its ear.

"(Peter, Andrew, you blue-collar fishermen) **Follow me, and I will make you fishers of men."** (Matt. 4:19)

"James, John, you're not old enough to own your own business but you're old enough to follow me." (Mt. 4:21)

"(Matthew, you evil, reviled tax collector) **Follow me!"** (Mt. 9:9)

"Rich young ruler, sell everything you have. Give it to the poor. You'll have treasure in heaven. Then come, yes I'm talking to you, follow me." (Mt. 19:21)

See, Jesus says in John 15:16, **"You did not choose me, but I chose you, and I appointed you, that you should go and bear fruit..."** He chose you. He picked you. He called you. He commissioned you to live a fruitful life! It's as if he's saying,

"You may not think you have what it takes to become the person I created you to be, but I do. I know you. I made you. I wove you together in your mother's womb. I know what makes you tick. You can live a fulfilled, complete, and abundant life. Now, YOU may not think it but you're letting your past, and your guilt, and your shame, and all this other garbage weigh you down and hold you back.

"You know what? When you asked me to forgive your sins, I did. So draw close to me, walk in my forgiveness and follow me to that river of

living water. I chose you because I know there's something special about you."

Jesus went out and got people like me. He went out and he got people like you. And the religious community got all over him. They said he was a friend of sinners. They called him a glutton and a winebibber (Mt. 11:19) because he went down into the dirt. He went down into the mud. He went down to the people that needed a physician. He grabbed us and he lifted us up and he cleaned us off and helped us become the people he created us to be. Stop letting your guilt and your shame and your past keep you from fulfilling your potential.

The Bible is full of people like you and me, just a bunch of screw ups who in our own strength can't even find water. But when we allow God to fill us and make the most of us, we can change the course of the culture…in spite of ourselves.

WORTHY IN HIM

Think about David, for example. Many of us look at David as the standard by which other kings are measured. David was a man after God's own heart, after all. Surely David wasn't a screw up…was he? Well, the Bible says, *"The thing that David had done was evil in the sight of the Lord."* (2 Sam. 11:27) Evil? David?

You can read it for yourselves in 2 Samuel chapters 11 and 12 but here's the Readers Digest version. David sends his troops out to battle while he stays home. One morning he looks out his window and sees a hot woman taking a bath and since he was the king he has his men bring her to his castle. He takes her against her will. She becomes pregnant. He tries to cover up his sin by having her husband sleep with her. But her husband, Uriah, was a dedicated soldier and refused to enjoy the comforts of home while his men were in battle. So David orders Uriah to the front lines where he's killed and David takes Bathsheba as his wife. It was all very neat and tidy and none of it escaped the eyes of the Lord.

David is soon confronted with his sin by the prophet Nathan, but instead of having Nathan killed and keeping the lie going, David falls on his face and repents before God. He writes of his sin in Psalm 51, *"I know my transgressions and my sin is ever before me...create in me a clean heart, O God, and renew a steadfast spirit within me...for thou dost not delight in sacrifice...or burnt offering...The sacrifices of God are a broken spirit; a broken and a contrite heart, O God, thou wilt not despise."* (3, 10, 16-17)

David was not a perfect man. But he was a giant when it came to repentance. Listen, God's not through with us just because we screw up. *"We've all sinned and fallen short of the glory of God."* (Rom. 3:23) The trick is not allowing our sin, guilt and shame to shackle us to a wasted life. Instead let's take a lesson from David on how to overcome our past.

CONFESS OUR SINS

I need to accept the responsibility for my sin. God didn't cause me to reject His plan for mine. That was my decision, *"Each one is tempted when he is carried away and enticed by his own lust. Then when lust has conceived, it gives birth to sin; and when sin is accomplished, it brings forth death."* (James 1:14-15) Trying to hide from my sin is senseless since it follows me everywhere and when the lights are out and the TV's off and nobody is looking, my sin surrounds me like a wet blanket.

The good news is that if I will confess my sin God will remove it from me, *"As far as the east is from the west, so far has he removed our transgressions from us."* (Psalm 103:12) But more than that God has also promised that if I humble myself before Him and take responsibility for my sin he will come into my life and help me clean up my heart, *"If anyone loves Me, he will keep My word; and My Father will love him, and We will come to him and make Our abode with him."* (Jn. 14:23) He will remind me everyday that I am no longer a sinner but a child of the King, *"Therefore you are no longer a slave, but a son; and if a son, then an heir through God."* (Gal. 4:7) (See also 2 Cor. 5:17 & Eph. 2:4-10) Confessing my sins frees me up to enjoy the fellowship of my Creator.

REPENTING OF OUR SINS

There's a pretty gross verse in the Bible that goes something like this, *"Like a dog that returns to its vomit so is a fool who repeats his folly."* (Prov. 26:12) I know it's pretty disgusting but it happens all of the time, doesn't it? How many people have you known who have been delivered from one addiction or another only to end right back up in rehab? Or maybe you know of someone who's been paroled from jail only to be arrested a short time later. Confessing our sins is a great first step but if we want to stay out of the vomit we have to change our eating habits.

In John chapter 8 we read about a woman who is caught in the act of adultery. This was a stoning offense at the time and the Pharisees who brought her forth wanted Jesus to lead the way. So after taking a look at the woman, Jesus leans down…but instead of picking up a rock he begins writing in the dirt. I don't know what he wrote but I have an idea he was writing down a list of sins, maybe the secret sins of those who were watching. Before long the older men began to walk away. Then the younger men. Soon Jesus is left alone with the woman and he says, *"Woman, where are they? Did no one condemn you?* And she said, *'No one, Lord.'* And Jesus said, *'Neither do I condemn you; go your way. From now on sin no more."* (8:11-12)

The point is Jesus is not about condemnation. Sin is condemnation enough. Jesus is about freedom. He knew her sin was keeping her in bondage. He wanted to free her to eternal life. And he wants to do the same with us. In order to do that we not only have to take responsibility for our sin but do our best to avoid it. *"Like the holy one who called you, be holy yourselves also in all your behavior; because it is written, 'You shall be holy, for I am holy.'"* (I Pet. 1:15-16)

If you're living in sin, if you're going through Hell, stop and turn around. Start walking toward the light, sin no more and accept his forgiveness.

ACCEPT HIS FORGIVENESS

You do know how far the east is from the west, right? They never touch. When we confess our sins and repent before God *"He is faithful and righteous to forgive us our sins and to cleanse us from all unrighteousness."* (I Jn. 1:9) God has already forgiven us. The problem is we have a hard time forgiving ourselves. Somehow we need to come to the understanding that nothing we do will increase our value before God. The Bible says, *"All our righteous deeds are like a filthy garment."* (Is. 64:6) But still he chose us. He picked us. And he died for us. It's his love for us that gives us value. Plus, if we allow him, God can use our faults and failures to *"perfect, confirm, strengthen and establish us."* (I Pet. 5:10) In other words, with His grace, our mistakes might actually helps us become the person God created us to be. I know it sounds unbelievable but maybe instead of dwelling on the impossibility of it all we should just try thanking him. Like Paul said, *"Always give thanks for all things in the name of our Lord Jesus Christ to God, even the Father."* (Eph. 5:20)

MOVE ON and STEP OUT

Finally, and this may be the hardest step of all, after we confess, repent and accept His forgiveness we need to move on in His grace. The apostle Paul said, *"One thing I do: forgetting what lies behind and reaching forward to what lies ahead, I press on toward the goal of the prize of the upward call of God in Christ Jesus."* (Phil. 3:13-14) Sometimes I think we get so biblically minded that when we read that verse we assume Paul is just talking about the miraculous stuff he's done…because he's Paul. But Paul screwed up, too. And I think he's telling us not to revel too much in the positive nor dwell too much on the negative but instead press on toward the bigger and better things God has created for us to do, in Him.

Confess your sins. Repent of your sins. Accept his forgiveness and move on. Don't let your guilt or your past keep you from becoming the person God created you to be. Remember, you didn't choose him. He chose you. (Jn. 15:16) You have been made worthy through Him so that you can accomplish great things for him!

Chapter Nine

Ready, Aim...Patience

"Patience is the companion of wisdom."
                                                        -St. Augustine

"Why is God taking so long?"

Good question. It's a question I get a lot in churches where I speak. I'm not sure I have the right answer since I think the answer differs for different people. But I think if we spend a moment or two on the question that might help us with the answer.

Why is God taking so long? We're not a people who like to wait, are we? I read a statistic on my TV show one day from the National Center for Health Statistics that showed nearly 20% of all live births are now induced. That's up more than 10% in just ten years. While I'm sure there are a myriad of reasons for this increase, convenience likely tops the list. I'm not sure I have a problem with that but it does seem to fit in well with the landscape of our culture; instant messaging, speed dialing, quick refunds...microwavable minute rice. This "drive-thru" mentality has us all believing that we can pull up to the window of life, put in our order for peace, love, and happiness and drive away without ever having to expend the least bit of effort. But isn't there something to be said about waiting?

How long do you think it was between the time God realized Adam was lonely (Gen. 2:18) and the creation of Eve? (2:22) Most of us assume since it was only a couple of verses that it happened just like that! 'Snap!' But in his book, <u>Searching for God Knows What,</u> author Donald Miller postulates that Adam may have waited quite a bit:

"But here is Adam, the only perfect guy in the world, and he is going around wanting to be with somebody else, needing another person to fulfill a certain emptiness in his life. And as I said, when God saw this, He did not create Eve right away. He did not give Adam what he needed immediately. He waited. He told Adam to name the animals." (pg. 63)

Miller goes on to explain that since Adam had to give names to *"all the cattle, and to the birds of the sky, and to every beast of the field"* it might have taken him nearly 100 years to name and categorize the millions of species God had brought before him all before God gave him what his heart desired. (Gen. 2:18-20)

I'm not saying I agree totally with this idea and I'm not smart enough to get into an argument over whether or not the earth was created in seven 24-hour days. But it does seem a pretty fantastic chore to name every creature in just one day. Yeah, I know God brought the animals before Adam but how did he get the whales into the garden? Wouldn't Adam have to make at least one journey to the sea?

My point here is about patience. God doesn't always give us what we want when we want it. In fact scripture seems pretty consistent that waiting is an essential ingredient in God's plan. I thought about this the other day while I was driving home from a revival service.

I know this admission may get me in trouble with a few people, namely law enforcement types, but I must confess that sometimes…I write while I'm driving. Now, I don't recommend this practice to anyone and I don't do it to prove how well I can multitask, it's just that, well, inspiration hits me at the strangest times and I've discovered that at my advancing age unless I write it down I'll lose the thought forever. So as I was headed home this one evening I pulled out my journal and scribbled down this thought, *"refer fo thus they am no pathology"* or something like that. The road was a little bumpy. But after some careful deciphering after I got home what I actually meant was more along these lines:

"Imagine how tough it must have been for Jesus to wait 30 years to begin his ministry. He came to save the people he loved and created and yet he has to wait.

In Luke chapter 2 we see Jesus as a young boy, left alone in Jerusalem, seeking out the spiritual leaders of his day, listening to them and asking them questions. He was learning all he could in order to prepare himself for his future task. He was preparing himself for his moment. It took 30 years for that moment to come to pass but each day he prepared himself for his calling.

It's tough for so many of us to wait for our calling. We want the job right now but we're not ready. We should focus instead on His kingdom and His righteousness and when the time is right we'll know it."

OK, I added a few words here and there but the thought is the same. Jesus came to earth with a mission and much preparation was needed before he was ready to fulfill that mission. At the wedding in Cana we see Jesus hesitant to perform even the simplest of miracles because as he says, *"My hour has not yet come."* (2:4) Timing and preparation is everything even for Jesus.

And there are other examples of this, such as Noah. In Genesis chapter 6 God tells Noah, a righteous man, to build him an ark because he's going to destroy the world. So Noah goes about gathering enough wood and materials to build a boat big enough to hold all the animals on the planet and then he waits for the rain…and waits…and waits. All the while he endures taunts and jeers from his former friends who think the old man is crazy since they have never seen or even heard of rain. And then one day, more than 100 years after the promise, that first drop of rain hits the dry ground. (Gen. 5:32 & Gen. 7:6)

Abraham is another good example. God promised Abraham he'd be the father of many nations (Gen. 12:1) then waits a quarter of a century before making good on that promise. (Gen. 12:4 & 21:5) Abraham wasn't very patient then and we're probably even less so today.

Sometimes we get in such a hurry to "do something" that we step out in our timing rather than waiting on God. Moses is a good example of someone clearly not yet ready to handle his calling.

In Acts 7:23 Luke tells us that when he was near the age of 40 Moses felt the calling, jumped in without so much as a whisper to God, and suffered the consequences. It took another 40 years of seasoning in the wilderness before Moses was ready.

So how did Jesus get a handle on his impatience if indeed he was impatient? Though the Bible doesn't tell us anything about what Jesus did between the ages of 12 and 30 Luke paints a pretty good picture telling us twice in his second chapter *"the child continued to grow and become strong increasing in wisdom"* (40) and *"Jesus kept increasing in wisdom and stature and in favor with God and men."* (52) In other words before we think we can assume the responsibilities of our calling we first need to set our minds on growing in favor with God and men.

We can grow in favor with God by reading and studying His word so that we can handle accurately the word of truth avoiding worldly and empty chatter. (2 Tim. 2:15) We can pray without ceasing (I Thess. 5:17) so that we can more clearly understand the shepherd's voice (Jn. 10:27). We can fellowship with likeminded believers (2 Tim. 2:22) who will encourage us and hold us accountable (Prov. 27:17). And we can then put all that knowledge into practice (James 1:22).

We can grow in favor with men by giving of ourselves and our resources (Matt. 5:16), by working hard without complaining (Col. 3:23) and by treating other people as if they are more important than we are (Phil 2:3-4, Mt. 7:12) just to name a few.

The tragedies of impatience are clear: bad marriages, stunted growth, compromised integrity, broken dreams you name it. But what are the benefits of waiting on God? Martin DeHaan of RBC Ministries writes that patience leads to earthly benefits (Job 42:10), provides us a better end than the present (Eccl. 7:8, Rom. 2:6-7), allows us to bear fruit from seeds of faith (Lk. 8:15), wins the approval of God (Ps. 40:1, 1 Pet. 2:20), makes us a good example for others (2 Th. 1:4), perfects our character (Jas. 1:4), provides us with God's power (Col. 1:10) and enables us to inherit God's promises (Heb. 6:11-12).

The benefits of waiting truly outweigh the consequences but that doesn't make waiting any easier, does it? Waiting is something we have to learn. It's a step-by-step process of successes and failures. Just keep reading and praying and growing and trusting and soon *"the God of all grace, who called you to His eternal glory in Christ, will himself perfect, confirm, strengthen and establish you."* (I Pet. 5:10)

Jesus tells us our first responsibility on this planet is to seek His kingdom and His righteousness and he'll take care of the rest in his timing. (Matt. 6:33) Stepping out in our own power, in our own timing and before we're ready is a good way to get disillusioned and frustrated. Not stepping out at all is a good way to rob ourselves of the abundant life God created us to live.

Section 3

Paradigm Lost

Chapter Ten

The Role of the Modern Day Church

"If we are the body why is His love not showing them there is a way."
-Casting Crowns

Several years ago I met a woman we'll call Kate. She had a passion to reach all those people who worked in the same strip mall that she did. So she talked to a local restaurant, reserved a room, lined up a speaker, put flyers up every where she could then prayed. She prayed that God would touch the hearts of those who saw the flyers and that she would have a good crowd. And she did! When the day finally arrived the room was packed with men and women, workers and customers all coming together to enjoy a good meal and hear a testimony about the love of Jesus Christ.

Kate was ecstatic and couldn't wait to share with her church what God had done. But the response was less than enthusiastic. Instead of sharing her exuberance Kate's pastor chastised her for not going through the proper protocols to put on a luncheon like that. She should have taken the matter before the missions committee, he said, and used some of their approved material. He even questioned the credentials of the speaker. Instead of applauding her passion and encouraging her outreach the "church" took exception to what they called her lone wolf approach. Disillusioned and hurt Kate eventually left her church. I'm not sure what happened to that strip mall ministry.

In his book Revolution, George Barna describes people like Kate as 'revolutionaries.' He says right now there is a *"growing sub-nation of people, already well over 20 million strong who...have no use for churches that play religious games, whether those games are worship services that drone on without the presence of God or ministry programs that bear no spiritual fruit...They are seeking a faith experience that is more robust and awe inspiring, a spiritual journey that prioritizes transformation at every turn, something worthy of the Creator whom their faith reflects...settling for what is merely good and above average is defeat."* (13-14)

Have you ever felt like there's got to more to the Christian life than the one you're living? Have you ever in a moment of solitude wondered if this was the life that Jesus died so that you may live? If so, you might be a revolutionary...or a barbarian. Erwin McManus writes that barbarians are driven by *"love, intimacy, passion and sacrifice...For them God is life, and their mission is to reconnect humanity to Him."* (The Barbarian Way, p.13) The problem is these barbarians *"are not welcome among the civilized and are feared among the domesticated. The way of Jesus is far too savage for their sensibilities. The sacrifice of God's son, the way of the Cross, the call to die to ourselves, all lacks the dignity of a refined faith."* (p.15)

I'm writing to you today as a barbarian, a revolutionary, or as Robert Lewis might say a 'go-person.' I know first-hand the dissonance that occurs when you try to share your passion with those in the church. I've seen the blank stares and the patronizing smiles and felt the cold water being poured on my head. I completely understand why many in the body today feel they have no choice but to pursue the upward call of God in Christ in spite of their church rather than with its blessing and support.

But it's important to understand that it's never been my desire nor do I feel it's the desire of most pursuers to go it on their own. I mean, when you're on the front lines of the battle you realize more than ever how much you need the entire body. I would have loved to have been discipled, mentored, encouraged, and supported by my church. But that didn't happen and it needs to.

The paradigm of the early church was for the body to reach people where they were, mentor and disciple them then release them back into the world to do the same. That paradigm has been lost, replaced with a safe, comfortable alternative focused on attracting others to our building then burdening the staff with the responsibility of developing programs to keep them from jumping to another building. The result has been an alarming rate of pastor burn out and a severely disillusioned, unfulfilled and increasingly irrelevant body.

Folks, we must embrace the revolution, but…

"MOST PASTORS DON'T TRUST THEIR PEOPLE WITH GOD'S WORD" –name withheld

Before I wrote this I sat down with a number of pastors who shared with me some very interesting insights. I can't share all of them with you but I do want to dwell on a couple of them since they were so often repeated. The first is that most pastors today don't trust their people with God's word. Many leaders feel that without proper supervision their unschooled members will quickly sell out to the cults or the liberals or the "emergents." The second, which may be a result of the first, is that most pastors today are trained by their seminary to be in charge of everything in the church.

But is that the paradigm that was set up by the early church? The apostle Paul said in Ephesians 4:11 & 12, *"He gave some as apostles, and some as prophets, and some as evangelists and some as pastors and teachers…"* Why? *"…For the equipping of the saints for the work of service to the building up of the body of Christ!"*

In other words the job of the leadership of a church is not to do all of the ministry themselves but to instead empower the body to fulfill their own ministries. Again, Paul says, *"The whole body…is fitted and held together by that which every joint supplies, according to the proper working of each individual part,"* which in turn, *"causes the growth of the body for the building up of itself in love."* (Eph. 4:16)

We each have a role to play. It's a role given to us by God to be worked out while we're here on earth. Finding that role is difficult and it's made even more so when the body is not allowed to explore their calling. If a pastor or church leader feels it's his role to spearhead all of the ministry in the community he's quickly going to burn himself out and that's exactly what's happening today. Did you know the average tenure of most pastors now is about four years? _(Today's Pastors by George Barna pg. 36)_ The Schaeffer institute reports that more than 1,500 pastors leave the ministry each month due to moral failure, spiritual burnout or contention in their churches

But shouldering the burden of ministry is not just devastating to pastors it's also crippling the body. Barna reports in his book <u>Revolution</u> that half of all believers say they do not feel they have entered into the presence of God or experienced a genuine connection with the Savior. Most churched Christians believe that since they are not gifted in evangelism that such outreach is not a significant responsibility of theirs. And the typical churched believer will die without leading a single person to a lifesaving knowledge of and a relationship with Jesus Christ.

In his book, <u>The Church Unleashed,</u> Pastor Frank Tillapaugh says much of the problem is due to what he calls the 'Spirit vs. Structure' approach. _"The structure-first approach,"_ he says, _"is one in which the structure is set and whatever ministry it spits out, the church does. That's much different from a ministry-first approach. This approach says if we have the people who want to perform a certain ministry; we will build a structure around them."_ (pg. 73)

Going back to the story I shared about Kate's strip mall outreach I wonder what would have happened to that ministry had her pastor or other church leaders congratulated her effort. I wonder where that ministry would be if instead of pointing out its flaws the church would have hooked her up with a mentor and through encouragement, bible study, and accountability discovered ways to make the ministry even more effective. If there's one thing I've learned over the last seven years of trying to inspire, encourage and motivate others to fulfill their ministry it's that nothing can take the place of passion. Building a structure around the Spirit is much easier and more effective than trying to start a fire from scratch…especially if the wood is wet.

Yes, there will be failures when people first step out of the boat. It's not natural to walk on water…but it's not impossible either! And it may be the only way to heal the body.

As I've mentioned earlier I had no intention of going it alone in pursuit of the ministry to which I believe God had called me. But that's what happened. And that's what continues to happen to so many people today; people who don't want to rock the boat but know that in order to satisfy the burning inside of them they've got to take a step out of it. And to paraphrase Bugs Bunny, *"That first step…is a lulu!"*

But even the bravest and the boldest need a little encouragement. Here are a few things I wish the church had been able to give me as I wrestled with the decision to get off base and back out onto the playground.

1. Embrace the Revolution. Henry Blackaby has said we need to *"find out where God is at work and join him there."* Well, God is at work in the revolution and sooner or later the organized church will have to make a decision to either embrace it or fight against it. But why on earth would you choose to fight against a movement of people that strongly desires to put their faith into action? These are people who no longer want to go to church but to be the church. Isn't that what we want? If the modern day church hopes to remain relevant they need to humble themselves, step out of their old wine skins and consider supporting even encouraging those crazy, out-of-the box, revolutionary ideas the Spirit has given some of their members.

2. Lead from the top. Everyone sitting in those pews has been woven together by God for a reason. They need to hear the message preached as often as possible that each and every one of them are expected to put their gifts, talents and abilities into

action. But not only do they need to hear this message preached they need to see this message modeled before them. They need to see the pastor crossing denominational lines to support another church's community outreach. They need to see the leadership actively supporting a members desire to launch a ministry of their own and they need to know how they can turn their own passion into reality. I read recently of a church that added to their staff a "release pastor" whose job it is to help others fulfill their ministry. What a great idea!

3. Disciple, Mentor and Celebrate. When a believer approaches you with a crazy idea for starting a Sunday morning ministry at the local golf course, don't laugh. God has asked his children to do some pretty crazy things over the years, hasn't he? And besides, there may be a lot more men at that local golf course Sunday morning than in your pews. Instead of looking for the ice bucket to fill and pour over their head begin a regular schedule of discipleship. Find out why he feels that way. What scriptures led him to that revelation? Discuss the pros and cons of starting a ministry with an eye on encouragement. Then celebrate the victories. My feeling is that you may soon find you don't have enough hours in the day to help all those people who are having crazy visions so it might be helpful to train and mentor other leaders who can train and mentor other leaders and so on, and so on, and so on…

4. Have ministry fairs. As your outreach begins to grow begin to schedule ministry fairs on a regular basis. Many pursuers will be gone on Sunday morning and some may not know why. This will give everyone a chance to see what the body is doing, add credibility to the ministry effort, give some an opportunity to get involved and may inspire others to summon the courage to step out onto the playground and into their own ministry.

5. Don't fear failure. Many pastors are well-meaning shepherds who want to protect their sheep from danger. But danger is a

part of the journey. Many of us have no idea how to follow Christ and failing is a great teaching tool. For over a year I tried to do God's work my way and nothing worked. When I was at rock bottom the only place to look was up. That's when God began to work. Our natural tendency is to roll up our sleeves and help wherever and whenever we see a need but let the Holy Spirit guide you. Don't be too eager to step in and prop up a brother or sister who is struggling. Think of it sort of like a Marine boot camp. That drill instructor has to disabuse that raw recruit of years and years of thinking only about himself. He will shout. He will work. He will tear down that recruit. Then begin the process of building him up and changing his way of thinking in order to be part of a team. One day he may have to put his life in the hands of others and they may have to put their lives in his. That trust isn't natural. It's developed through discipline, training and trial under fire. Give God the space to do the same thing with your members.

6. Financial and administrative support. It might surprise you that this is last but had I received regular financial support before the mentoring and discipleship it would have killed my ministry. Still, most of us who enter into full-time ministry have no idea what we're doing and could use a little...no, a lot of advice; legal help, administrative help, leads on prospective donors, putting together a donor support package all would be much more helpful before the first check comes in.

Those are just a few ideas to help you embrace this revolution. I'd love to hear more if you have them as I'm sure I'll have more suggestions after this goes to the printer but let me take a moment before we leave here to try and calm a couple of your fears as church leaders. The first, while we're on the subject, is financial.

One thing I've learned about pursuers over the years is...they're givers. They know their money is not their own. They know everything they have is to be used to further the gospel and that includes their possessions. I know people who've given away vehicles. They've given large monetary gifts though they couldn't afford it. They have garage sales to give money to others going on mission trips. Pursuers are incredibly generous. They're even, by and large, big tippers! How about you?

But pursuers give as God directs. They give where the needs are and yes if they feel their local church is more concerned about monuments than ministry their giving may go elsewhere. Now, this is not done out of spite it's more out of sorrow as they see the incredible potential of the church being wasted. That being said if pursuers like myself see their church beginning to move in the direction of the revolution they will support it with their tithe. Though I'm at my church on average one out of every five Sundays they get my entire tithe...and much more since I have kids in the youth group! And I know of other pursuers who do the same. I know it may not make much sense that the people who aren't in church are doing more to support the church but have you ever known God to make much sense? Stop worrying about the bottom line. Or rather seek first his kingdom and his righteousness and trust him to take care of the bottom line.

Another thing that may have you a little concerned is that if you encourage your members to go...they will. But that's OK. Remember, we're not in competition. Think of it this way, pursuers are actually expanding the ministry of the church. Tillapaugh tells of how on Sunday mornings they typically had only 200 or so in church but once a year they would have a "church-wide" celebration on Sunday morning at the Seventh Day Adventist church (they meet on Saturdays) and fill up all 1500 seats. In other words while there were only 200 people "at church" on a typical Sunday the overwhelming majority of members were "doing church" throughout the community at strip malls, apartment complexes and maybe even golf courses. Their focus was not internal but external and as a result their ranks exploded.

But something else may happen as your outreach explodes. You will attract other pursuers. See, I have a feeling it may be a while before other churches catch on to the revolution but as more and more people are filled with the Spirit more and more people will be in dire need of support and encouragement. If they see that one particular church is embracing the Spirit they'll be drawn likes moths to a flame.

Crazy, isn't it?

A FINAL WORD...AND A WARNING

Jesus said that when he comes back again in all his glory he will separate the sheep from the goats putting the sheep at his right hand of favor and power. The sheep will be in that position, he says, because when he was hungry they fed him. When he was thirsty they gave him something to drink. They took care of him when he was a stranger, naked, sick, or in prison. But many of the sheep will say, *"Lord, when did we see you hungry and feed you or thirsty and give you drink?"* And Jesus will answer, *"Truly I say to you to the extent that you did it to one of these brothers of mine, even the least of them, you did it to me!"* (Mt. 25:31-40)

The sheep didn't even know they were ministering to Jesus. They just...ministered. They let their light shine before men performing their good works even to the least of these and bringing glory to God in the process (Mt. 5:16). The goats on the other hand probably considered themselves sheep. They said, *"When did we see you hungry or thirsty or a stranger or naked or sick or in prison and NOT take care of you?"* (44) The sense I get is that the goats most likely would have ministered to the least of these if they knew Jesus was among them after all he was kind of important. He was worth their time. Helping him most likely would carry some reciprocal benefits. But those other folks...they just aren't worth the effort.

Do you want to see a good picture of what a goat looks like? Turn over to Luke 7: 36-50. Here, Jesus is invited to the home of a Pharisee who failed to provide water for his feet, gave him no formal greeting and didn't anoint his head with oil. Yet at the same meal there was a woman. A "sinner" who from the moment Jesus sat down began wetting his feet with her tears, wiping them clean with her hair then kissing them and anointing them with perfume. And what does the religious man say about all this, *"If this man were a prophet he would know who and what sort of person this woman is who is touching Him that she is a sinner!"* (39)

You know, many religious people think they're sheep because they host a nice dinner party for Jesus or a potluck or just go to church on Sunday morning. But if you've ever referred to someone as "one of those people" or "that sort of person" and look at them with scorn rather than as someone in need then you need to be concerned about which side you're on.

Who are the least of these? And just what is our responsibility to them? Calvin and Fee Fee Jones know the answers first hand.

See, twice a month Euphemia "Fee Fee" Jones walks from her front door to a makeshift kitchen her husband Calvin built a few years back and begins cooking. But she's not cooking for the two of them. From a pantry stocked with food from Arkansas' Rice Depot and other ministries and with the help of about 10 to 15 volunteers Fee Fee will cook for and deliver meals to more than 800 senior citizens and shut-ins throughout the city of Warren and Bradley County, Arkansas.

But the Jones' love for service goes beyond just cooking. The stories in South Arkansas of their charity and kindness are legion. One such tail includes the editor of the local paper who says after news got out that he and his wife were 'expecting,' Fee Fee demanded he get over to her house right away. When he did she made him accept a box packed full of diapers and other new born needs.

Now, tales of charity like this are rare but not uncommon until you consider that Calvin and Fee Fee have a take home income of less than $1,000 month. That becomes clearly evident when you visit their home. The walls are buckling, the foundation is sinking and the ceiling is porous. Last year a group of volunteer builders from the local Baptist association came by to try and see what they could do to help but the condition of the house was so bad all they could do was put tarps on the roof and pray for God to intervene.

But Calvin & Fee Fee never complain. They never make excuses. Even though two of the four burners on their stove don't work and they have use a 2 by 4 to keep the door on their industrial oven closed they get their meals prepared every other Saturday and deliver them on time to the hundreds of people who have it a lot worse off than they do.

Calvin and Fee Fee are truly remarkable people and it's impossible to be around them without being inspired to do more for the kingdom. But, one day I had lunch with a man who lives in Fee Fee's home town. He attends a church in her denomination. In fact he's a leader in that church. Yet he confessed to me over hamburger steak and mashed potatoes that until I brought it to his attention he had no idea of the scope of their ministry.

I didn't say anything at the time since he was paying for lunch but I'm sure he saw the look of befuddlement written all over my face. I mean how could 800 people in a town of just over 6,000 receive meals from a woman in his denomination and the church not know? Could it be that the type of people ministered to by Calvin and Fee Fee are the type of people most of us in polite church don't like to think about? I'm sure if Jesus came back we'd pull out all the stops. We'd have pot lucks and cantatas and live manger scenes. But again, *"To the extent that you did it to one of these brothers of mine, even the least of them, you did it to me."*

You know, I hope I'm wrong but I think it's only a matter of time before churches across this country lose their non-profit status. I know that sounds impossible but the rumblings have already begun.

During the budget battles of 2009 President Barack Obama proposed decreasing to 28% the rate at which families earning more than $250,000 a year can deduct their charitable contributions. While this may not affect those of us who don't make anywhere near that kind of money what is clear is that the government needs cash and contributions to churches and charities are a prime target. Now let me be clear this is not about politics rather it's a warning to churches that the salad days are coming to an end.

It's important to understand the reason churches were given their tax deductible designation in the first place. Following the tenets of Christ churches existed to clothe the naked and house the homeless and feed the hungry. The motivation, of course, was that by addressing the physical needs of the people the church would later earn the right to minister to their spiritual needs. (See Matt. 5:16, John 9) This gave the body purpose and meaning, satisfaction and contentment as each member using their God-given talents performed their good works and brought glory to the Creator. The government granted to those who donated to their churches the privilege to deduct their contributions because the body of Christ was providing a valuable public service.

But following the Great Depression when the government began to step in and increasingly meet those social needs the body of Christ began to retreat. After all, the need was met, right? The void was filled, wasn't it? Why duplicate the services the government is providing? Soon those tithes and offerings the churches had always received were spent not externally but internally. Church buildings grew larger but the bodies outreach withered as did its significance to the point where today millions upon millions of "believers" have to buy a book to tell them how to find purpose in life.

These days many churches provide no community benefit at all. Sure, they teach and encourage moral uprightness and provide salve for the battered soul but what good is all that knowledge of right and wrong if when *"a brother of sister is without clothing and in need of daily food... you do not give them what is necessary for their body. Faith,* James wrote, *if it has no works is dead, being by itself!"* (James 2:15-17) Too many fellowships across this country have become noisy gongs and clanging symbols. (I Cor. 13:1) We're collecting money from the members but instead of meeting needs we're building multi-million dollar family life centers to insulate ourselves from the very people we are commanded to serve. And the government is noticing.

While you may not care about whether or not "the rich" get to deduct their contributions you should be aware of the next logical step. As the state expands its outreach to the poor it will require more and more money. And churches appear to be flush with cash as evidenced by the explosion of monster sanctuaries springing up along most major highways. And if you're listening you can begin to hear the growing roar of protests from the public when another church announces its plans for expansion. Chewing up real estate while not providing anything in return eventually will mean only one thing; your tithe is next.

When we as the body relinquished our role to the state we turned over the spiritual well-being of God's creation to an entity that could care less about it. I know there are those in public office with the best of intentions but the simple fact is the government is more interested in securing power than restoring lives. Unless we wake up to the fact that we've abandoned our mission and refocus our time, energy and finances to reclaim that mandate we will lose our favor with the government. Then again, maybe that's not such a bad thing. Maybe a little persecution is just what we need to restore us to favor with God.

By the way, it might interest you to know that once Calvin and Fee Fee's story came to light; our ministry was able to organize a building campaign. Dozens of God's people came out from all across Arkansas to tear down their old run down shack and within two months provide them with a brand new 3-bedroom, 2-bath home…with a great kitchen!

Chapter Eleven

Now What?

"It's kind of fun to do the impossible."
-Walt Disney

"And walking by the Sea of Galilee, he saw two brothers, Simon who was called Peter and Andrew his brother, casting a net into the sea; for they were fishermen. And He said to them, 'Follow Me and I will make you fishers of men.'" –Matt. 4:18-19

So, are you still thinking, "If God's going to do something big in this county, in this state, in this country, he's going to have to do it through somebody else?" Are you still saying things like, "I'm too old, I'm too slow, I'm not sharp enough, or I live in this little bitty town out in the middle of nowhere?" Listen, if that's the case then you've already shut off the power of God before He's had a chance to get His hand on the faucet! All He needs is a willing heart. All He needs is someone who says, *"Here am I. Send me."* (Is. 6:8) Or, *"Be it done to me according to your word."* (Lk. 1:38) Or even, *"Who is this uncircumcised Philistine that he should taunt the armies of the living God?"* (I Sam. 17:26)

Have you ever heard of a town called Bethsaida? It's actually one of the most frequently mentioned cities in the New Testament but if you're like me you probably skip right over it on the way to something more important without ever stopping to consider the significance of this little town.

See, Bethsaida was a tiny little fishing village on the edge of the Sea of Galilee. It was situated right next to the cities of Capernaum and Chorazin and made up sort of a tri-cities area where Jesus spent a lot of time and performed more than a few miracles. In fact, many scholars today, such as Dr. Rami Arav of the University of Nebraska, who actually rediscovered Bethsaida in 1987, call this area "the evangelical triangle" because of its impact on Christianity.

Anyway, Bethsaida, while significant, wasn't very large. In fact it was populated by only a few families, maybe five to seven, but those families were pretty extended. See, back then when someone would get married the father would simply add a room onto his house and the new family would move in and the house would get larger. This is why when Jesus said things like, *"In my Father's house there are many dwelling places"* (Jn. 14:2) the people of his day knew exactly what he was talking about. By the way, kids…don't even think about it!

So with this small family foundation, Bethsaida had a population of only about one or two hundred. But do you know who came from Bethsaida; Peter, Andrew, James, John, and Phillip. That's almost half of the disciples. Almost half of the disciples came from a tiny fishing village on the edge of the Sea of Galilee! But these guys, these blue collared fishermen, changed the course of history. How? They allowed the Holy Spirit to fill them up and make the most of the gifts, talents and abilities He gave them in the first place. And if it can happen in Bethsaida it can happen in your town, too.

Remember, it's not you, it's Him. And if He could start a revolution with a bunch of smelly fishermen in Bethsaida you better believe He can do something with you, too, right where you are. The question is: Do you want it?

Do you want the explosive, abundant life that Jesus promises in John 10:10?

You call yourself a Christian but do you really want to be a follower of Christ?

Are you willing to take a chance to sell everything you have, give your treasure to the poor and come follow Him? (Mt. 19:21)

You say you believe in God but do you believe God?

Do you believe He will strongly support you? (2 Chron. 16:9)

Do you believe He will meet your needs according to His riches in glory? (Phil 4:19)

And do you believe He will perfect, confirm, strengthen and establish you? (I Pet. 5:10)

You know what? The life you were created to live is being held in trust right there in the palm of His hand. But in order to grab hold of that life, the life you've always wanted, you have to be willing to lose yours. (Mt. 10:39) No one gets the abundant life, no one gets to that river of living water, and no one gets to those green pastures on their own terms. In order to become the person God created you to be you have to follow Him.

And He is way off base.

About Beautiful Feet Ministries

Beautiful Feet Ministry was founded in 1998 and incorporated in 2001 as a 501 (c) (3) non-profit ministry intended to inspire, encourage and motivate the believer to be all God created them to be.

The ministries of Beautiful Feet include CrossHeirs Sportsman's Fellowship, Utility Man Community Service Outreach and the Little Rock Media Fellowship. You can find out more information by visiting www.beautifulfeetministry.com

About Matt Mosler

Matt Mosler is a television and radio personality, syndicated columnist, speaker and singer. He is also an ordained minister and the full-time director of Beautiful Feet, Inc.

Before becoming the morning news anchor for Little Rock, Arkansas' NBC affiliate, KARK, Matt spent most of 20-plus year career in television as a certified meteorologist for TV stations in Alabama, Mississippi and Texas before finding a home in Arkansas.

Matt speaks and sings more than 100 times a year conducting revivals, retreats, youth events, wild game suppers and concerts for churches, schools, corporations and civic groups. He has recorded two CD's. This is his first book.

Matt has been married to Camille since 1989. God has blessed them with three wonderful children: Travis, Madison & Rebecca. They love living in Sherwood, Arkansas.

To have Matt speak at your next event or to order more books please contact him at:

matt@beautifulfeetministry.com

LaVergne, TN USA
23 March 2010
176931LV00003B/97/P